THE JOURNEY OF AN ACCREDITED PROVIDER

ANGELA H. BAYER-PERSICO

Back photo by
JANE SANTOS PORTRAIT
Foreword by
DAWN CRAMER, FORMER NAFCC ACCREDITATION
MANAGER

PLF Press

Second Edition

Published by PLF Press an EduMatch® Imprint
PO Box 150324
Alexandria, VA 22315

ISBN: 978-1-953852-06-9

These books are available at special discounts when purchased in quantities of 10 or
more for use as premiums, promotions, fundraising, and educational use.
For inquiries and details, contact sarah@edumatch.org.

CONTENTS

Dedication

I dedicate this book to my children, Gabriel, Peter, John, Caterina, and Vincenzo. May you always feel and know how much I have loved you from the moment I knew I was pregnant. You have been my inspiration and reason for all I have done in my life. Wherever life takes you, remember your roots and fly strong and hard.

To my partner, best friend, and husband, Giovanni. I thank you for the support, love, and understanding you have given me. This book would not have been possible without your encouragement and patience as I relived so many memories. You are my rock. I love you with all of my heart and soul.

And to Jack. I will always remember you. I miss you, and thank you for encouraging the birth of this manuscript. Thank you for being a great friend.

Love always,
__Angela__

Foreword

At the heart of it, National Association for Family Child Care (NAFCC) accreditation helps you be better. In a very intrinsic and holistic way, it unlocks your potential. Those of you who have a true passion for accreditation see it. After all these years, what I think I am hearing from you is, accreditation gets to the heart of quality. It takes everything we know about what is good for children ... just add RELATIONSHIPS. Easy peasy, right? The magic is in the box! Well, we all know the real truth. It really takes hard work to get there. Family childcare is an innately beautiful, strong, and loving field. Hold on to your standards, and you will never have to compromise that.

I love NAFCC accreditation because it empowers you to new levels—often levels you never even knew were in you. I can hear it in a provider's voice when I'm on the phone. It's an underlying astonishment and empowerment all at the same time. "I DID IT!" And, of course, most of you are so professional with us, but I know you squealed a little bit at least and some a whole lot, even if only inside and even if it was your seventh accreditation. You know I am talking to YOU. Every time I sit there wishing SO BADLY I could see your face in that moment, beaming with pure joy! I don't know if we will ever truly have the data behind that, but how can you deny it?

That is all I ever heard in Angela's voice all those years as we spoke on the phone and emailed back and forth about her accreditation. Dedication and love were at the heart of her work. She even called to notify me when she had to move and let her accreditation go. I heard the loss and sadness in her voice about closing her childcare program.

When she came back to accreditation years later, all I remember is that Angela handled herself always with the utmost grace. It was not until I read Angela's story that I truly understood how much grit and passion she put into her work with children. This is an incredible journey.

-from the heart of a former NAFCC accreditation manager
Dawn Cramer

To My Readers

- For all providers who work diligently—day in and day out — with our children. Thank you.
- For all teachers, making an effort every day and bringing work home every night—thank you.
- For all educators, putting the students first even while dealing with personal struggles—thank you.
- For all teachers, logging 50 plus hours a week while still making room in your hearts for each child—thank you.
- For all providers, caring for infants as if these babies were your own—thank you.
- For all educators, opening your businesses with extended hours and weekend hours—thank you.
- For all parents who cannot find quality childcare, it does exist.
- For all parents who want to give up on childcare, look into National Association for the Education of Young Children (NAEYC)-accredited and NAFCC-accredited facilities.
- For parents experiencing horrible moments with childcare services, I am truly sorry. Your child is the most precious little human ever and deserves all the respect and love possible.
- For teachers, the "little engine" *could* because he *thought* he could. Childcare can always be improved. It is up to directors, supervisors, teachers, support systems, and assistants to make childcare a service that parents trust and feel comfortable turning to.
- And finally, for everyone working in childcare, we need to break the "babysitting" mentality the public holds regarding our purpose and prove that we are so much more.

May this book bring inspiration to your lives.

Love,
Your author,
AHBP

1

NAFCC CONFERENCE 2017

I LOOKED AT MYSELF IN the long wall mirror in my hotel room in Alabama. I was getting myself ready to walk over to the National Association for Family Childcare's (NAFCC) annual conference in July 2017. A second glance in the mirror showed me a woman in a semi- business-looking, brown dress with enough makeup to look decent and yet enough to cover up the bags under her eyes, the ones that revealed how tired she was.

My long, dyed-brown hair was worn straight, loose, and back. I wore a name tag: Angela H. Bayer-Persico, Accredited Provider. Below the name, it stated Presenter. Although this woman was me, I hardly recognized myself. I am a presenter. I have knowledge to share through experience and education. I am accredited through hard work and dedication. This is my story. I am here to tell you how I made this incredible journey to becoming an accredited provider and presenter.

Everyone's journey in life has different tides and unexpected twists. If I could have predicted the future, I would have known which path might have led me to happiness quicker and which would have led to endless sorrow. Each choice and decision in my life has made me who I am and got me where I am now. I do not regret any decision. Instead, I look back and am grateful that I have been blessed and loved throughout my life. I have had angels come into my life when I needed them.

THE DECISION TO START MY CHILDCARE BUSINESS

I STARTED MY JOURNEY INTO my childcare business back in January 1999. I looked into turning my one-family house in Stroudsburg, Pennsylvania into a family childcare home. My reasoning was simple: I was a mom of two with one on the way, and childcare for three children was going to be costly. Many home childcares start this way. I was employed as a caseworker at this time and knew quite well the expense of childcare for three children. Sixty to seventy percent of my salary would go to childcare. Mostly though, after interviewing many childcare places listed in the classifieds and at my local childcare referral service, I felt uncomfortable leaving my children with any of these providers.

I toured childcares that were dark with poor lighting, with old, even broken toys, dirty yards, smelly kitchens, and no books or art areas. One had a huge dog—much bigger than my 110-pound pup—in the middle of the childcare space. I love animals, but such a large dog in a small room was asking for children to be knocked over—it wasn't a question of whether the dog was friendly or not at that point. Another provider I interviewed greeted me in her pajamas at 5 p.m. Either she was ready for bed too early or never bothered to change clothes for the day—unprofessional and unprepared, in my opinion. I don't think that I was asking too much.

There was one childcare home that had many children in the living room watching cartoons on TV. I didn't know anything about regulations and ratios regarding childcare, but it seemed like nine kids in her living room was a lot. Other childcare homes had strong cigarette odors, like they had just put out the cigarette before I rang the doorbell. The search was depressing. I wasn't looking for a babysitter. I wanted someone to play with my boys. I interviewed centers and found some nice learning environments, but they were far, out of the way, and very costly. I was living in rural Pennsylvania, so choices were very few. I couldn't find a family childcare home that I liked or felt comfortable with.

I wanted professionalism and an inviting, stimulating, enriching, and safe environment. I did not think I was being too picky. Maybe, just maybe, I could do this myself. How hard could it possibly be?

BEGINNING THE CHILDCARE PROCESS

W ITH NO FAMILY OR FRIENDS to rely on for childcare, I had to consider my idea very seriously. I ordered a copy of the licensing regulations and read through them. The regulations made sense and could be very applicable to my situation. Consequently, I went through the application process and submitted the required state paperwork to open a childcare in my home.

I completed Child and Adult Care Food Program (CACFP) training to join the program. The program covered recommended foods, allowable foods, and the food guide pyramid in a new way. I learned to cut grapes into fourths to prevent choking. I learned that every meal needed specific portions—child-size portions. I would have to serve a fruit and vegetable with every lunch and dinner in addition to a protein and a carb. It helped me rethink my *own* food choices.

* * *

Angela's Advice

The CACFP is a fantastic service because it helps providers offer healthy food to all children. After my business was off the ground, I was partly reimbursed for two meals and a snack that I served the children during the day. I say partly because I would serve three meals and two snacks to the children every day and my cost for the food was always higher than the reimbursement rate. Despite this shortage, I still loved the food program. They offered free annual trainings and support for any questions that I might have about food.

WITH SO MANY different socio-economic differences and varied thoughts on "healthy" choices, the CACFP program made it possible to serve the same nutritious food to all children. I preferred this process because I had noticed at "Mommy and Me" programs that some parents brought in fruit gummies as a substitute for actual fruit or even Chef Boyardee instead of a homemade pasta dish. I wanted everyone to be served the same food, unless they had certain food allergies or kept a kosher diet. I made it a point to become nut-free even though my own family, including me, loved peanut butter. I wanted to prevent an anaphylactic shock with any child as much as possible.

After completing and submitting the applications, I waited for the inspector to assess my home.

Angela's Advice

Regulations may vary from state to state, but here are some of the standard requirements that an in-home provider is expected to fulfill:

- State orientation Application fee State inspection
- Background clearances
- TB test for provider and all household members over the age of fourteen
- Health department inspection of water and sewer Playground inspection
- Furnace inspection
- Medical clearance by doctor First aid and CPR training
- Infant sleep-safe class and a shaken baby syndrome class

* * *

WITH ALL THESE REQUIREMENTS, no wonder there are so many unlicensed childcares in operation. Now that I knew the regulations, I was surprised that some of the places I had visited were allowed to operate. Maybe their registrations had expired, and I had not noticed. Or maybe no one inspected them frequently. My county had more than 80 family childcares. Only one inspector covered three counties. I could understand why infractions slipped through the cracks. Now, I was on the inside and seeing things from the provider's perspective.

All was in order, and I got my registration to operate a family childcare in my home on July 16, 1999—the day before my birthday and just three weeks after giving birth to my third son. (In Pennsylvania, they do not issue licenses to family childcares, they issue registrations.)

4

WORKING AS A CHILDCARE PROVIDER

BEING A MOM OF THREE and having taken care of my children's cousins multiple times, I felt more than competent to run a childcare. It was normal for me to be caring for four or five children on any given day. I foresaw that my business would be like a normal working day for me. How hard could it possibly be to take care of several more children who were strangers every day?

Piece of cake.

One night after receiving my registration, I lay in bed, and I started to think. Do I write a handbook? How do I write a handbook? How do I charge people? How do I make sure they pay? Are late fees allowed? How do I get clients? Where do I advertise? This was going to be different. I was no longer taking care of younger cousins or a neighbor's child. This was a job. I was going to be taking care of other people's children. Strangers. Complete strangers were going to be coming into my house and interviewing *me* to see if they felt comfortable leaving their most precious and valuable little human in *my care.*

Despite the weight of the responsibility, I decided a verbal agreement was good enough. I thought it best that the process be informal and friendly, not procedural. I was telling the parents what my policies were during the interview, while I was still trying to figure out my policies. One rule I made clear: smoking and guns were not allowed on the premise. I also asked that each parent supply their child with their own diapers, wipes, and extra clothing. Pretty basic.

I was looking at it from a mom perspective, not a businesswoman perspective. I had no business background or business education. My past experiences caring for my own children and their cousins gave me confidence to do this work. Unfortunately, I had no experience working with parents. I was only following my instincts. I trusted that I would be able to work with the parents because I knew the parent perspective.

Now, I was on the other end—people were coming to me and expecting me to know how to run a childcare. With this in mind, I looked at the interview process in a new light. I wanted to make the families feel like they could trust me and feel comfortable about leaving their children with me. My goal became to make my home "their home away from home."

I wanted to offer the professionalism and inviting environment that I had sought for my own children. With a pat on my back, I looked around my setup. The three childcare rooms were on the first floor of the house. I organized my play areas in a way to make the environment welcoming, fun, and inviting. I turned my living room into the main playroom. It was the first room that visitors saw when they walked in. This room featured a small music center with my piano and percussion instruments: toy drums, maracas from the dollar store, two tambourines, and a xylophone. A corner was crammed with stocked bookshelves—hardcover children's novels, Golden Books, and Disney books featuring princesses. On the opposite corner from the books was a space full of blocks. I set up plastic crates with different block types—wooden blocks and Legos—many of these items my boys had recently outgrown.

My dining room featured a 12-person table that also featured an art area and science center. I had shelves filled with crayons, markers, paper, paints, and brushes in the art area on one side of the room. The science center on the other side of the room hosted a shelf with science books, a plant, a bug habitat, and some magnifying glasses. This room was also where the children ate their meals. My hutch with my good china was in the dining room. In-home childcare meant that my business shared space with my furnishings and family in my home. When I hosted my own family dinners on weekends, we would move the "school" shelves onto the porch to make the dining room feel less like a childcare.

The third childcare room was the den. This area served as a nap and changing space. I kept the nap mats behind my couches and blankets in bins on the side. I had all the children's extra clothes placed in labeled cubbies in the den. I had a diaper-changing pad that I placed on my couch when I changed the diapers. It seemed like everything was in order.

The childcare took over the house. I was glad, though, that my older boys had their own space in our fun, finished basement that was every kid's dream: pool table, air hockey table, foosball, basketball hoops, arcade games, and video-game system. The basement was their perfect hang-out spot. My boys needed their own space because the childcare was visible everywhere on our first floor. Their bedrooms were on the second and third floors of the house and inaccessible to the childcare.

My first interview was memorable. A parent called asking about childcare openings. I cleaned my home until it was spotless. I was very nervous. I had a lot to be nervous about because I had already given my boss notice that I was not returning after maternity leave. When they came in for the interview with their child, I had this feeling that I needed to be a hostess. In other words, I felt like I had to offer them coffee and snacks and sit down and talk about me. I did not have any professional background taking care of children, so all I could do was talk about how I cared for my boys and their cousins, along with my work with special-needs children. I had no handbook, no policies. I did not know where to start, so I had not written anything yet. Guidelines —written or verbal—did not seem necessary. And what could the difference possibly be to accept children without any? Little did I know.

The mother asked me for my hours. I told her that I was available to help her out at any time. She asked for overnight and weekend care. I was available. What else was I doing? I needed clients, and I needed to start somewhere. Service prices were not differentiated among day, night or weekend care nor by age. My thinking was that I was taking care of a child in the same manner, regardless of age. I set my rates at almost half below the going market rate in the area in order to get clients. I started by caring for an eight-month-old along with my own one-month-old in addition to my older two boys. I did not charge a registration fee or establish a late policy. I did not think that I needed them. I followed the clients' pay schedule, meaning I would get paid every two weeks after the care had taken place. Clients set my policies and hours based on their work schedules, not the other way around. At this time, I had no idea how many mistakes I was making.

Because of my positive thinking and generous offerings, I started getting clients. I was full in less than a month! In my care, I had six children, including my infant son John in addition to my two school-age children. I observed an open-door policy for all registered parents. I tried making sure that each child got to know me and I got to know the families. In order to be accommodating, I was open 24 hours a day, seven days a week. Extremely hard hours, but I needed to bring in the clientele.

Stroudsburg was known as a commuter area. Parents would drop off as early as 4:00 a.m. and head into New York to work and return to pick up their children as late as 9 p.m. I also had second-shift parents working at the local hospital, so their pickups would be around midnight. Planning menus and creating a topic for the day, along with cleaning (and more cleaning), were among the daily chores in my work schedule. I had no breathing room because my days were filled with the childcare and my own children.

5

FIRST BUSINESS PROBLEM

W ITH ALL THIS ORGANIZING, TOPIC planning, and cleaning, I forgot about the business part of my work. When my first client told me she could not pay me because her car broke down and she needed to pay the mechanic, I told her she could pay me from her next paycheck in two weeks. I did not have the backbone to say otherwise. I did not want to lose a client. Her following payday also presented a problem because her hours at work were cut. Consequently, I was not paid again. For four weeks now, I had not been paid. This was a problem. I was human, and I understood that life can take some bad turns, but now I was working for free. After the fifth week, this client wound up losing her job, and I lost the client. I also lost five weeks' worth of pay. As a newbie, I felt taken advantage of because I trusted her. The fact is, I let this happen. I didn't even have a contract in order to take her to small-claims court to get reimbursed. And I did not even have the time because I would have to take off work to go to court and hope to get reimbursed. I had only myself to blame.

There was no one I could talk to about this problem. I had no co-workers or colleagues or other adults to talk to during the day—no sounding boards to get me through this issue or any other issues. Three months open and I already had business issues. It was a lonely, isolating job, working from home by yourself with only children to talk to all day.

This was a new venture, and I learned how people could easily take advantage of me. And I had no idea how to set up policies. I needed to set some rules, but I had no starting point. It was up to me to create my childcare policies.

I started writing up a family handbook with rates, hours, and posted events on the daily schedule. In the handbook, I also offered my background. It was two pages and not much of a handbook, but it was a start. I explained the services I provided and what was expected from the parents. Pretty rudimentary, yet I felt like I was actually running a business. My first client had taught me the necessity of some policies. I look back at that experience and am grateful it occurred early into my childcare business days, not later. I learned by my mistakes. I changed my fee policy to make payments due on Monday or the first day of care, not the last day of care. This assured payment at the start of my services.

The universe, knowing I needed help for my childcare, sent me mail from a local college advertising the Family Child Care Credential. This certification was exactly what I needed, but returning to college was not what I had in mind at that point in my life. I already had gone through college for a Bachelor of Arts degree. As a full-time childcare owner and mom of three boys, I did not see how this could be possible. Tuition was another factor. I read the brochure from Northampton Community College with the course information and realized the courses could be taken online. OK, now that was something I could handle. However, the cost was still prohibitive. I learned then about a scholarship from T.E.A.C.H., a federal program, would not only cover tuition, but books and my time. I would get paid for all the time invested in studying and taking the course! That was a huge incentive.

No excuses now. I signed up for the next semester and went back to college using my dial-up modem and computer. I completed online courses during nap time and after my own boys went to bed. This was the best decision that I ever made. This decision set me on the path of education, and I learned how to improve the quality of my business. One of the most important things I learned was that I had fooled myself, thinking I knew how to run a business. I can look back now and ask myself, what was I thinking? I was so naive when I started. I was grateful I had gone back to school.

To open my childcare, all I had needed was a GED or high school diploma, the proper space, and to follow the fairly simple state regulations for health and safety. After becoming familiar with all the Pennsylvania state regulations, I realized that none of these regulations explored topics of business professionalism, including how to write a contract. The Family Child Care Credential taught me all the basics I needed to run a business. (I continued my early care education studies throughout the years to eventually earn my master's degree in Early Childhood Education 12 years later.)

6

INTRODUCTION TO NAFCC

FTER A COUPLE YEARS IN business, I received a mailing from the National Association for Family Child Care (NAFCC). I skimmed through the information regarding NAFCC and membership. I wondered why I should join. I read the description about the accreditation briefly on the NAFCC website. I now had an associate's degree in early childhood. No one at my local college was familiar with accreditation for family childcares, and there were no accredited family providers in my county I could question. I had no mentor to turn to for answers. Unfortunately, the bottom line was that financing the accreditation process was also a problem.

I had earned my Family Child Care Credential. That was enough for me, I thought. I mentioned the accreditation process to an acquaintance. She asked me why would I want to pay for a rubber stamp if I thought my business was running well enough. I agreed. I did not really understand the meaning of accreditation. I did not research it. The flyer got misplaced with some files on my desk. I never threw it out. Now and then, I would see this flyer on my desk and wonder about accreditation.

I got involved with my local NAEYC board (National Association for the Education of Young Children) as the only family childcare provider. I sat on the board and networked with directors and other educators. Through them, I heard about a pilot project called the Keystone Stars. It was a rating system for childcare centers similar to the restaurant or hotel rating systems. I found that four stars was the highest rating, and accreditation made your childcare an automatic four stars. The NAEYC accredits large centers. I spoke with accredited center directors. It was enlightening. Accreditation meant you were working at a higher standard of care and offered true quality to families.

I started my research into NAFCC. Accreditation had been around for more than 15 years. This organization had a firsthand understanding of what it meant to work with children in the home. Per the NAFCC website: "The National Association for Family Child Care (NAFCC) is the only professional association dedicated specifically to promoting high-quality early childhood experiences in the unique environment of family childcare programs. NAFCC works on behalf of the 1 million family childcare providers operating nationwide." That's a lot of dedication and understanding on their part. Who better than NAFCC to help me do my job better? It definitely made me see NAFCC in a different light.

During this time, I got a call from a prospective client, inquiring about my hours and rates for "babysitting." I told her I was not a babysitter but, in fact, I taught young children through play. The caller's attitude made me want to scream: "I AM NOT A BABYSITTER!" But how could I explain that to them? This potential client responded by asking how much TV the children watched. I said none. She explained that her child had learned his numbers and the alphabet through TV shows and, therefore, all he needed was a good educational show. (She also insisted again on calling me a babysitter.) She insisted that her child watch TV at my childcare or she would not sign him up. (She never did sign up.)

I will never forget this caller. She made me realize the only way I could make people see my services differently was to go through the accreditation process. If I did not want to be seen as a babysitter, I needed to offer a high-quality early childhood program. Using savings, I requested the self-study guide and got started. This was a huge step in my career. I thought it was going to be a simple stamp of approval of my work, but it was so much more. The standards made me reflect carefully through different eyes. It was enlightening to learn how much I needed to change and revamp. My work became more focused. I used the self-study guide to its full potential and learned to improve myself and my business. It did not occur overnight. I spent a couple of years working on meeting the standards.

I was hesitant when it came to the parent surveys. This is the part of the accreditation process where each client in my program answered questions about me. What would they say about me? My inner voice told me if they trusted me with their kids, they had to like me and would say so. All parents needed to fill out a survey and either return it to me in a sealed envelope or mail it to NAFCC directly.

In order to get an idea about how to improve, I placed a quality improvement suggestion box on top of the sign-in sheet, and I let the parents anonymously drop notes in a box. This helped ease my fears. I also learned to self-assess even better. I used their suggestions to improve my business, and my job became easier. I learned to take their suggestions, not as critiques, but as suggestions for improvements. I discovered it was so much more than just having the right environment or aesthetics. I needed to form professional relationships with the families. Quality improvements lay in my communication with parents.

7

NAFCC QUALITY STANDARDS

Accreditation defines what the quality benchmarks are in family childcare and are an important resource for local and state organizations as they create quality-rating systems.

— SUZANNE GESSNER WILLIAMSON, "INSPIRING
OUR FUTURE"

T HE NAFCC VALUES STRUCK A chord in me. They advocated for quality childcare and a true commitment to the profession of childcare. The membership meant I was part of a larger group of family childcares that wanted to provide quality childcare. The Keystone Stars program in Pennsylvania was using the NAFCC standards as part of the basis for the standards.

The accreditation process examined all aspects of the family childcare program: relationships, the environment, learning activities, safety and health, and the professional and business practices.

The application process was intense and very detailed, but clearly explained.

I started with the self-study, where I reviewed and studied each quality standard. It was meant to be a living self-study that continually evolved to ensure quality care.

The Family Child Care Project at Boston College's Wheelock College of Education and Human Development led the development of the NAFCC accreditation system in a thoughtful, organized, and systematic process. Providers, parents, resources, and referral staff, along with other childhood experts, all collaborated in the creation of the standards. The different perspectives from these collaborators allowed for the standards to be valuable, applicable, and meaningful.

The following are just some of the quality standards found in the self-study and how I met them or evolved as a provider and teacher through the process:

EXCERPTS FROM THE STANDARDS

NAFCC accreditation standard: The provider cares about, respects, and is committed to helping each child develop to his or her full potential.

Each child had to be shown the same commitment of care and respect. This was at the core of my work—respectful caring. As the first standard, it was the most important one. If I did not respect or care for the children, then why bother proceeding with the self-study guide? Why work in this field if I was not committed to helping each child be who they could be? Children are little humans with feelings and emotions. It was up to each teacher to help them discover themselves. Children are not objects to be talked down to, ignored, or dismissed.

I needed to interview a prospective employee to help me as a substitute. I had never been in a position to be a boss or to hire anyone. As a new business owner, I only knew to follow my gut about hiring. I met the woman, who was very polite. She entered a room full of children, but did not seem to really see them. She was more interested in talking about herself and her credentials, which is all well and good, except that she ignored the children. I gave her the tour. One child was on her belly on the floor, looking at a book. She stepped over the child as she kept talking. Another child was standing by the doorway, building with Legos. Instead of respectfully excusing herself, she picked up the child to move him out of her way as she continued to speak about her qualifications! I knew right then and there she was not a person who was respectful or caring of children, regardless of her outstanding credentials or references. Children are not objects. We would never think of moving an adult out of the way.

NAFCC accreditation standard: The provider seems to like children and to enjoy being with them.

I loved getting up in the mornings, did not dread Mondays, and did not grow impatient waiting for the last child to leave. I honestly wanted to be with the children. In the past, I had jobs when I could not wait for the end of the day. I repeatedly checked the clock waiting for 5 p.m., so I could punch out. I could not relate to that anymore. I looked forward to every morning. I awoke with a smile on my face, knowing I was making a difference in a child's life. Childcare became part of my life. When I went shopping, I would not only look for things for myself, but for my class. Even my own boys knew I appreciated things for the class, and they would get gifts for my childcare students for Mother's Day or my birthday. My birthday gifts would be music CDs, children's books and educational toys. I valued these items more than flowers!

There was a pride in working with children. I truly loved my job. I got to spend time with my own boys all day and be there for them after school, too. My youngest child had playmates all day. But it was hard work—draining and emotionally demanding—and certainly not babysitting.

NAFCC accreditation standard: The provider encourages parents to visit their children anytime. She is available to parents by telephone when their children are in attendance or she regularly checks for phone messages.

My open-door policy to all registered parents stated this standard. I had set this rule in place without knowing it was a quality standard of the NAFCC. I had this open-door policy with the parents because I wanted them to know that as long as their child was in my care, they were always more than welcome to join us. I remember picking up my two oldest boys at a childcare when they were younger, and I was made to wait for more than five minutes before the provider opened the door. Those five minutes dragged while my mind raced, considering the worst that could be happening. The delay gave me a bad feeling, and I did not send my boys back there again. I could hear children in the house, and the provider just told me to wait. There was no reason for me to wait while I heard her talking to the children. I probably would have called the cops if I had a cellphone, but this was before everyone owned cellphones. I was that worried. Consequently, I did not want the parents to have that same dreadful experience. That provider never gave me an explanation for the long wait. I was never allowed into the house either. My boys, at that time, were nonverbal, which made me feel even more uncomfortable.

One time, a parent called to ask me whether he could pick up his child early. I asked him, "You want to know whether YOU, the parent, can pick up YOUR OWN CHILD early?" I made him realize how silly his question was. He told me his previous childcare provider did not allow for pickup during certain times. I thought this was ridiculous. They are the parents and the guardians. Unless a court order restricts pickup, there is no reason why parents cannot pick up their own child at any time.

Angela's Advice

I understand it can be a disruption to the day to have parents pick up their child at different times, especially during nap time. But providers need to be conscious of parent's changing schedules. Look at it from a parent's perspective. Make them feel comfortable.

I WELCOMED parents at my childcare. As a parent, I appreciated the good feeling one experienced when greeted by a provider and teacher. Parents would come in and hang out for a cup of coffee or tea in the morning during drop-off. One parent came in to drop off, made his coffee and was asked by the class to read a book. Thirty minutes later, he was still reading to the class, and I just observed and enjoyed the interactions. Other parents made it their routines to help feed their children breakfast during the morning drop-off. I welcomed the help. Children were more comfortable with me because their parents were welcome there.

NAFCC accreditation standard: The provider keeps parents informed, by conversation or in writing, about their children's activities—daily for babies and at least weekly for older children.

I had conversations daily with parents about their children. I kept a written composition book log on each child, what we did, how they ate, what they ate, and even their bowel movements. Recording everything made sense to me because it gave parents a chance to observe their child's development and growth during their time with me. I knew I would like to know what my children did all day if they weren't with me. One parent commented that her child's logs were her child's dairy. Years later, I learned this parent had kept the logs as a keepsake.

These notes also served as reference points when something important needed to be noted. Children who were nonverbal could not express when they were not feeling well, but their eating and sleeping patterns said it all. The daily notes also helped to keep track of milestones and progressions. I used an assessment tool (Ages and Stages) to screen children throughout their growth and development.

I also made a photo journal for each child to record growth changes, learning activities, and fun events. I wrote anecdotal notes in each photo journal. Twice a year, during parent-teacher conferences, I would share these photo journals with the parents. (Yes, I did parent-teacher conferences. I was a teacher.) I needed to touch base with the parents and guardians about their children's development, growth, progress, and goals. I made these photo journals by simply printing out photos and inserting them into loose-leaf binders. (This was prior to the digital age.) My older boys helped me sort through the photos and set up the individual binders.

One parent told me she was glad to have photos of her child in an album. She had yet to print out any photos of her child because of lack of time. I got it. Time was a factor for all of us. I needed help. My "staff" (my boys) got used to filing and sorting artwork into mailboxes.

I would also write up a highlights report—a weekly summary of different activities with the class. These reports showed the families what their children were learning through play each day. For example, on Monday, the class ripped up paper, and during that activity, the children strengthened their fine-motor skills. The activity also aided in their learning to hold writing instruments because ripping a paper requires the same pincer finger positioning. My motto for my program was "Where Playing is Learning and Learning is Fun."

I made up monthly newsletters and calendars showing all special events, birthdays, and special guests. I celebrated every child's birthday with decorations and books as gifts. I invited the local police department, fire department, and nature center to join us. Parents were invited to join us for any special event.

NAFCC accreditation standard: The provider's family members are courteous and respectful when they interact with the childcare children and their families.

My children and husband were very respectful of my clientele. They understood the childcare was a way of life and our life. The boys were growing up as part of the childcare. They helped me with the cleaning chores, among other activities. They were my cleaning crew every day. I blended childcare activities with my own children's activities. My boys did homework at the same time all the school-age children did their work, and meals were eaten together. Eating dinner at 5 p.m. was our norm.

Gabriel, my son, dressed up as a magician and put on magic shows. He even perfected a magic trick by making John, my youngest son, disappear into a box. Peter, my second oldest, read books to the class after dinner. He read very animatedly. He made up games to play with the class outdoors, and we had fun. Peter had an innate ability to work with little ones. His future could be clearly foretold.

My husband was not involved with the children at all. He spent his days either in bed or in his upstairs office. (He was very sick with heart and back issues.) His nurses took care of him while I was working. I had no formal employees except for an occasional substitute or assistant.

NAFCC accreditation standard: The areas of the home used by children are welcoming and friendly, appearing like a family home, a small preschool, or a combination of the two.

I scrutinized my setup and environment. I crawled on the floor to obtain a child's perspective. I sat in each corner of the rooms and tried to imagine a better setup. I asked the children what they thought and valued their answers. It was their classroom. I observed their play and noticed traffic patterns, and made adequate changes. It was a small space, so I had to work with what I had and not make it overwhelming.

Balancing a home and business in the same space is tricky. The idea is to look "professionally homey." In the foyer, I placed a sign-in book, mailboxes for each child, a bulletin board, cubbies with coat hangers, and areas for shoes. And, as I described previously, the childcare space occupied the main floor, including my kitchen. These rooms were available for walk-through inspections at any time. I gated off my upper floors for privacy and stair safety. Family areas were on separate floors and allowed my boys and husband to have their privacy.

NAFCC accreditation standard: At least 10 books for children under the age of two.

These 10 books needed to be in good condition and age-appropriate. My board books were chewed up. I bought more books at the local library's book drive—for all ages and including various topics. I revised my rotating system because my shelf space was very limited. In addition, I did not want the children to get bored looking through the same books over and over, so my rotating system provided fresh titles. (Reading was a big part of my life, and my boys are all big readers. I would get complaints from Gabriel's teachers because they found him reading instead of doing assignments. I knew there were worse things that he could be getting in trouble for, so I never made a big deal of these complaints.)

In addition to replacing books, I had to get rid of some books. Princess books needed to be removed. I had a lot of those books—all books that portrayed stepparents in a bad light needed to go: Cinderella, Sleeping Beauty, Snow White, and more. With so many blended families, it was important not to paint the stepparent negatively. This was a new perspective for me. I grew up reading those fairy tales, but now I understood they could be destructive to those relationships.

I needed to add more multicultural books so children could see themselves reflected in the stories. Children needed to see more than a cute bunny or dog as the protagonist. They needed narratives that reflected their cultures and languages and exposed them to different cultures. As an example, most of the children in my care had never ridden a subway or seen skyscrapers. Consequently, tales about children in New York City were eye-opening for them.

The library had an outreach program with a bookmobile that visited childcares once a week. The bookmobile was a huge bus filled with books and comfy seats. It parked in my driveway, and we checked out many books on a weekly basis. I would request books, too, to help me extend the study and interest of the children for the month. This convenient literacy extension was a huge bonus for the class.

NAFCC accreditation standard: Children have opportunities to make choices and explore their own interests.

This standard meant I needed to be flexible with my agenda and lesson plans for each day. I really could not expect the children to follow a strict structure of a box-type curriculum. Box curriculums were condensed into themes and topics with ideas for everything. Parents loved them. They felt that their children were participating in something worthwhile because cute projects came home every day.

I felt "boxed" by these curriculums, though. They allowed no room for the children's interests and I was wasting time and money on these programs. I created my own lesson plans based on each child's interests, age, and family's input. Even then, these lessons could be overshadowed by a child's interest in a butterfly flying past him or a fire truck heading down the street. I learned about emerging curriculum and teachable moments, and then I implemented those.

Angela's Advice

Children need our help to learn social and self-help skills. Knowing how to blow their own nose, toilet by themselves, dress and feed themselves is more important than learning how to write their names or count. I learned we need to have our children earn a master's degree in playground fun and a doctorate in sandbox play in order to be ready for school. I teach parents about my play-based program and my philosophy during the interview time. Social skills and a child's social-emotional intelligence show a correlation with academic achievement later in life. Parents need to learn that ditto sheets (practicing letter/ number tracing) are nothing but crap sheets for children under 4.

* * *

NAFCC accreditation standard: Children have daily opportunities for small-motor activities, such as grasping, scribbling, cutting with scissors, buttoning, tying shoes, using art materials, or playing with manipulatives.

I had to ensure a specific time for small-motor skills. I scheduled puzzle time and made art part of the daily routine. I learned to let the children lead the art process and not be concerned about the product. Their artwork was not precut or premade for them—each was a child's "Picasso" work. I supported their proper use of scissors and rolling of play-dough. I talked to the parents about the importance of the art process and asked them not to expect perfectly pretty pre-cut pictures. Some parents held preconceived notions regarding artwork. I taught them that each scribble was an important mark to each child. Writing begins with scribbles and evolves into identified lines and circles. In addition, I labeled each piece of art with the child's name and the date to demonstrate each work was valued, and this showed the growth and development of their work over time. I placed children's artwork on the windows in the dedicated art space.

Angela's Advice

To add to my point regarding precut crafts and art projects, if I cut, paste, and display models to the children, they do not identify the artwork as their own. There is no pride in its ownership. There is no individuality. Crafts are cute, but I learned they have their place, and their place was not in my childcare. In addition, artwork should be displayed at a child's eye level with care and attention. Children are not robots, they are unique, so their artwork should not be cookie cutouts of each other's. Art should be owned by their child creator, not the teacher.

ONE DAY, a parent joined me during art time. She noticed how I took out supplies and how some children took out their own supplies. The children sat down and worked. And I mean, they worked hard. The parent sat down and joined the class. She saw her child drawing and cutting. She asked him what he was doing. The child answered, "I'm making flowers." The mother then cut out flower shapes from construction paper and added them to pipe cleaners. The child continued to cut and paste his flowers (random unidentified shapes) into his garden picture. He added glitter and stickers and used popsicle sticks as stems, not necessarily in a "perfect" order. When the mom was finished, she showed her flowers to the child. The child saw them and then looked back at his flowers and said, "Those are yours. These are mine, Mom." That child was so proud of his hard work. The mom learned to value the artwork after she observed the work, time, effort, and love her child put into his project.

NAFCC accreditation standard: Children have opportunities to explore the natural and physical environment, such as watching insects, planting seeds, caring for plants, playing with water and sand, and playing with balls.

After reading this standard carefully, I thanked my youngest son for his love for entomology and nature. John taught me to stop, observe and admire the smallest creatures. Creepy-crawlies were his love. I remember the first time he picked up a daddy longlegs when he was 2 years old, and I almost screamed at him to drop it. He had given me a questioning look. I realized *my* fears and *my* phobias were going to transfer to him just like they had to his older brothers. I needed to stop my squeamishness. I swallowed my fears and let John touch the creepy-crawlies. Soon enough, John was chasing his older brothers with a spider (or snake), and they would scream and run away while he laughed at them.

I did what I do best, I read and learned about bugs. In addition, when John was a little older, he joined an entomology group. (He spoke with snake charmers and learned to respect snakes.) Soon the front porch was crowded with homemade insect containers (empty rinsed out mayonnaise jars with a cloth fabric cover and tied with a rubber band). John filled these jars with creatures from his bug hunts. We also stored a large container of worms. Our menagerie grossed out some parents, but the class loved to peer into these containers and John taught the children about the different types of bugs. Eventually, both the parents and the children appreciated our fascinating collection.

An additional activity that recognized the importance of nature could be found in our vegetable garden. Every year, my sons and the class planted a vegetable garden that was more than 100 feet wide. Weeding this garden was a continuous monumental task. The deer, rabbits, and other wildlife feasted on the vegetables. We harvested in the fall and made delicious meals with the vegetables. The garden would yield baseball bat sized zucchinis. There was always a surplus of vegetables that we loaded into a wheelbarrow, then we walked to our neighbors to donate them. I created a beautiful sunflower garden, too. We measured these mammoth flowers while they grew and took photos, and developed them throughout the process. The class made photo albums to record the growth of the plants.

NAFCC accreditation standard: List of suggested materials.

The standard suggested toddlers have large and small developmental materials, such as equipment for climbing, riding toys, balls, large blocks, puzzles, and water and sand play. I bought more riding toys at yard sales and received some donations from parents. I bought balls at the Family Dollar store. Unfortunately, these lasted only one season. I used package boxes for large blocks. I decorated and then affixed contact paper to them for durability. I bought more challenging puzzles for older children, 3 to 6 years old. For the babies, I needed to buy balls. I found gripping ones and soft ones to be the best. I bought nesting, grasping, and stacking toys for the little ones, too.

The toys and equipment made sense, but it also meant I needed to redo what I thought was sufficient. I got acquainted with school catalogs like *Environments*, *Discount School Supply*, and *Lakeshore*. I saved a bit from each paycheck to put back into the business. I realized going cheap at the Dollar Store was not always best because of the quality, the type of materials used, and where the items were produced. I recycled boys' plastic restaurant cups for the little ones to use for stacking and playing. Creativity became second nature as a means of resourcefulness.

I researched prices for a sand table and a water table and determined they were over my budget. I decided to use large under-bed plastic bins for sand and another for water play. I spent a fraction of what it would have cost, and the children had the same learning experience. I was becoming practical, not necessarily by choice, but because of the lack of funds.

I had not realized other items in my childcare were dangerous. As an example, I needed to remove my childhood toy chest from the childcare space. It was a beautiful piece of furniture made by my father. However, it had no safety hinges or air holes. The accordion gate across the main area also was removed because the children's fingers could get caught in it. Future purchases were made with care and thought regarding health and safety.

I set up a mixed-age space, so everything in my childcare needed to be safe for all ages. NAFCC suggested adding sewing materials for preschoolers. I had not thought of this. I visited my local A.C. Moore store, and it donated fabrics, looms, yarn, and weaving boards it considered leftover pieces. I was accumulating a lot of new materials for my program, and I could not display everything because my space was limited. I started a rotation system with the materials and placed several bins in a storage space to clean up the look of the rooms. Monthly rotations allowed for different toys in the rooms and kept the children more engaged. This translated to happy kids who were learning through play.

NAFCC accreditation standard: Time-outs are used only as a last resort with children age three and older. Time-outs are cooling-off times, rather than punishments.

Time-outs and countdown methods for discipline were very common with many parents, and even teachers used a time-out to send a child to the principal's office. I saw misbehavior as a call for attention, a call for help, a cry for connection. The child is having a hard time, not giving me a hard time.

* * *

Angela's Advice

Instead of time-outs, I implemented "time-ins." When a child misbehaved, I had that child stay with me. For example, little Mary Jo (age 3) wanted to hit another child with a block. I sat with her and used concise words to communicate: "I cannot let you hit." I stayed with Mary Jo while the other children continued playing, and I modeled block play for her. I shadowed the child. This method helped prevent further hurtful instances and taught proper social skills. I used the first person to communicate— instead of "you cannot hit"— because she *did* just hit and she knew that she physically could hit. I let them know I could not allow hitting (or whatever the ꞏunwarranted behavior).

* * *

SCOLDING, demeaning, and cursing a child were methods I never used. I only raised my voice for dangerous situations. Here's an example: I found I had to raise my voice frequently around the swing set. An 8-foot space served as a safety zone, partitioning off the swing set. The children would play tag and constantly forget and run in front of the swings. I placed a low-rise wall, 8 feet around the swings, to stop the children from running into the swing area. The wall worked somewhat to offset the swing area. However, when a new child entered the program, I had to teach the safety-zone lesson again. After too many close calls and weighing the pros and cons of safety versus fun, I opted to donate the swing set. Best decision for my program.

NAFCC accreditation standard: The provider encourages children to express their thoughts and feelings and listens with interest and respect.

Feelings are neither good nor bad; feelings just are. Getting mad about a toy being snatched by another child is normal. (I know I would be angry if someone ripped a book out of my hands while I was reading.)

* * *

Angela's Advice

Just because children are little does not mean they do not have big feelings. Too often, I heard parents diminish their child's feelings by telling their child that "you're okay" after their child's building of blocks was destroyed. The child was crying and upset because their work was lost. As adults, we have learned to control our emotions. A little one's pre-frontal cortex is not developed until the age of 26, to be able to be able to control emotions and outbursts. Instead of diminishing children's distress when they were upset, I told children, "I hear you. It seems you are upset (angry, sad, scared)." And I stayed with them, repeating these phrases to let them know I was there for them. I gave them words to their feelings. Dismissing their feelings does not allow children to grow and learn from the experience. Children need to own their feelings, not let them bottle up, to allow inner growth.

* * *

NAFCC accreditation standard: The provider uses music in a variety of ways, such as singing, finger plays, clapping games, playing instruments, and playing a variety of recorded music.

THIS STANDARD WAS my forte because I was musically trained and had been a music teacher and therapist for several years before going into childcare. I could fully satisfy this standard. However, I felt I could learn more songs. I played the piano and sang with the class, but I wanted to use more improvised music. On my own time, I had to practice music to improve, and I researched more tunes to play and sing. I needed more than just Raffi melodies and the "Baby Beluga" songs. I desired to expand my children's repertoire of singers and songwriters.

At this point, I wasn't meeting the standards and checking them off a checklist. I was using the standards to learn where I could improve my services for the children. Self-study means just that: an introspective time to consider my work and make it the best it could be.

NAFCC accreditation standard: Children are not permitted to leave the program with anyone other than their parent or specific individuals designated by a parent in writing or verbally. This applies to noncustodial parents.

I reviewed my family handbook for my policies on pickup and added this standard. I also added that I required proper identification from anyone not known to me who was picking up a child. I had all parents sign off on this policy indicating they were aware of this change.

I would like to share a story regarding the enforcement of this standard. A great-grandfather, unknown to me, was allowed to pick up a child. The parent had added his name to the designated pickup list and had told me in advance the great-grandfather was picking up that day. The great-grandfather rang my bell, and I asked him for his ID. He looked at me like I had three heads. "Young lady, let me in. My great-grandson is here." Meanwhile, the child was behind me yelling, "Pop-pop, Pop-pop." Obviously, he was the great-grandfather. However, I needed to stick to my policy. I wavered and almost, almost told him it was OK. But, instead, I insisted I needed to verify his ID. The great-grandfather turned around and, using his cane, walked down my front steps, mumbling under his breath. After retrieving his wallet from his car, he returned and said, "Young lady, thank you. Not many people would have had the gall to make me do that. I trust you with my baby."

Who, but me, is responsible for checking identification? I was it. The responsibility was mine alone. I was the one responsible for enforcing my own rules. I had no supervisor. I was the boss and teacher. In this instance, it would have been easier to let the policy slide. I had found the backbone to stick to this policy, among others.

NAFCC accreditation standard: No toxic plants are to be within children's reaches, and the provider teaches children not to pick at plants without permission.

Children do not know any better, and they can easily ingest any plant. I learned that ingesting a flower, stem, or leaf of certain plants could lead to abdominal pain, difficulty breathing, paralysis, coma, and even death. In our yard, we had planted rhododendrons, azaleas, lilies, wisteria, hydrangeas, and many other beautiful plants and bushes. Some of these plants held toxins that could be dangerous. What was I supposed to do? Dig out the whole yard? I certainly did not want a child at risk.

Consequently, landscapers redid the front and side areas, making them child- and pet-safe. I had no choice. (Deer and other wildlife know which plants are dangerous, and they stay away from them. People add borders of daffodils to their flower beds because deer know to keep away from them.)

In addition to the above standards, the NAFCC offers injury prevention guidelines. One by one, I followed best-safety practices. Here are some examples:

- It became the norm to never allow balloons for parties, even my own children's parties. A balloon is not only a choking hazard to a child, but, if released, it could be a choking hazard to animals.
- The first-aid kit was stocked (restocked, if supplies were used) and checked monthly. I kept a log.
- I had the bathroom knob changed, so the children could not lock themselves in the bathroom. This made my guest bathroom non-private, but this inconvenience was necessary for safety reasons.
- Electrical cords were secured and out of the reach of the children. Blinds and cords were all put up. (I cut them short when realized I couldn't adjust them. The children came first.)
- Certified safety gates were installed. (I learned soon enough how to step over gates like a hurdler from a track team.)

I used a step stool, so the children could reach the sink easier, instead of picking them up to wash their hands. Little things really made a difference.

In addition to injury prevention, I made a checklist for nightly chores to ensure the bathroom and kitchen were stocked with paper towels and soap and the childcare areas were properly cleaned and sanitized.

I reviewed my policies, contracts, and family handbook. The standards demanded that I make many improvements for health and safety reasons. In addition, they forced me to scrutinize my daily work habits. I learned to set higher goals. I created a philosophy for my childcare, and I wrote it in the family handbook:

I wish to serve you by providing your child with a secure and accepting atmosphere in a stimulating environment. This program provides experiences that enrich and enhance each child's cognitive, language, social, emotional, physical, and creative developments. Within the center's daily schedule, each child has opportunities to create, explore the environment, and learn problem-solving and social skills through firsthand experiences. Opportunities for solitary play as well as group activities are provided. I warmly support and nurture each child, and I am responsive to each child's individual needs.

I also presented my mission statement:

Angela H. Bayer strives to encourage each child's individual capabilities and supports each child's emotional, social, cognitive, and physical developments through professional early childhood methods at this childcare. Ms. Angela works in conjunction with the parents/guardians and community resources to ensure high quality, individualized childcare at this facility.

After each standard was reviewed and reviewed again, I felt that I was working at my highest ability and meeting the highest possible quality in childcare. My work and self-study reflected these levels. It had been a long road, and I knew I was better for it. Whether or not I was approved for accreditation, I knew I had improved my work significantly.

An observer was assigned to come to my family childcare during a designated month on an unannounced date. She came and observed my work unobtrusively and watched without comment throughout the day from a corner of a room—like a fly on the wall. It was nerve-wracking to have someone standing in the corner, taking notes. I had no clue what she was writing. Did she like my setup? Did she like my activities? Did she like how I interacted with the children? I hoped so because I was doing my best.

During nap time, the observer asked me a series of questions from the standards. This day was like any other day at work. Children got upset for the same reasons they always did. I demonstrated how, with a level head, I handled all the different situations that happened during the day. She noted I prepared the breakfast and lunch meals in the morning at the same time, and dinner was cooked during nap time. I did not try to make the day any different from any other day by planning anything special or acting fake. (The children would have picked up on anything different and acted differently themselves.)

I waited for the decision from NAFCC. And waited. I realized then how much accreditation meant. I wanted to be accredited. I wanted to work at this high level of quality in my childcare. This accreditation would be the culmination of my efforts. I did not take this endeavor lightly.

8

VALIDATION

November 2004: I opened a large envelope from NAFCC. Large ones usually meant good news. It was. I achieved my accreditation. I felt validated and elated. It was happy dance time, complete with whooping and yelling. I was ecstatic. This goal was one I had worked hard for. I was proud of who I had become. This was way more than a general stamp of approval. This meant I offered the highest quality childcare in my county.

I took my family out to dinner to celebrate. We enjoyed a nice seafood dinner at a local restaurant. My boys were learning how hard work pays off. I hoped that, professionally, I was an example to them.

My program had changed dramatically since I had opened five years earlier. I truly knew so little when I started, yet I thought I knew so much. Now, years later, my childcare enjoyed these elements:

- A regular clientele and a waiting list
- A stimulating and enriching environment
- An actual handbook, including philosophy, mission statement, code of ethics, background, goals for activities,

schedule, emergency plans, medical plans, fire safety drill plans, and much more. It was more than 30 pages long.
- Contracts, a termination policy, family background questionnaires, medical policies, and consent forms for photos and program activities (Some of these forms may be found in Appendix.)
- A thorough interview process
- Records of what I did with the children all day
- References for prospective clients

My oldest son Gabriel had his birthday party at home that year. His classmates were all invited. One of his classmate's parents was a reporter at the local paper, and they wound up talking to me about the accreditation process. Anyone who walked into my home knew I ran a childcare. There was evidence of it everywhere. After learning I was nationally accredited, the classmate's father asked his editor to run a story on me. I was the first to reach this status in Monroe County, Pennsylvania. This was the first of many stories that ran in the Pocono Record about my childcare. I was very nervous to do interviews, but finally, finally, there was good news about childcare.

I am tired of stigmas regarding home childcares because of the news. Every week, someone has hurt a child in childcare, and the news covers these stories on the front page. Stories of abuse are exactly why I did not leave my children in the care of a stranger and why I started my own childcare.

The reality is that parents need to work. Society has a structure, and childcare providers are an intricate foundation to this structure. With my accreditation, I was glad that, for once, there was good news about childcare.

9

LIFE AFTER ACCREDITATION

A FTER MY ACCREDITATION, I CONTINUED to value my time and work, ensuring continuous quality childcare. I changed the policies in my family handbook, and my weekly hours decreased from 24 hours, seven days a week to 50 hours, five days a week. I closed on all federal holidays. This change was prompted by a parent asking for childcare on Thanksgiving. The parent asked me what my plans were for Thanksgiving. I told her I was hosting my family. I thought we were simply having a conversation about the holiday. She replied, "So, you are home. I can bring my son to you, so I can have dinner with my boyfriend's family." NO. That was not acceptable to me. I could understand if she needed to work, but not because she wanted to go to her boyfriend's house without her child. NO.

I needed time off with my family. My family and childcare spaces were already mixed together, so I needed my time. In five years, I had not taken a day off, much less any vacation time. The reduction in hours would help, and I decided to add paid vacation time during the summer. I was worried parents would balk at my new schedule, but they did not. They understood regular hours and vacation time as

49

natural progressions in my high-quality work. It felt wonderful to implement these changes to my program policies, as well. I could not have changed them without my accreditation because some parents may have questioned why *they* should pay for *my* time off. Other jobs offered paid vacation time. I deserved it, and only I could ask for it.

The approval from NAFCC made it possible to further improve my childcare. The Keystone Stars program awarded me a four-star rating based on my accreditation. They also gave me a bonus grant for the childcare, which I quickly used to buy shelves and learning toys for the children.

In 2006, I applied to The Terri Lynne Lokoff Child Care Foundation for a grant. This grant was part of a National Teachers Award program that required a lengthy application and letters of recommendation in order to be considered. I never expected to be considered, and yet, I was one of the top 50 teachers chosen for this national award. I traveled with my family for the award ceremony in King of Prussia, Pennsylvania.

I enjoyed a complete makeover and a professional photo session. An incredibly delicious dinner was followed by the awards ceremony. It was a memorable night. Goodie bags brimmed with items for the class, plus $500 for my grant project ("Brilliant PAGER") and $500 for myself. I bought the class a comfy couch with built-in bookshelves on the back, and plenty of puppets and books.

The awards ceremony was featured live on television. I will never forget my fear of walking across the stage in front of cameras to receive my award. I was very nervous to be in front of a large crowd of people. By nature, I am an introvert. I do not like crowds or attention. I kept saying to myself: "Please don't trip. Please don't trip." I walked up the steps in beige, 2-inch heels and a light tan, knee-length lace dress with a pearl necklace to receive my Teacher Award certificate. I never made it to the center of the stage. I tripped on who knows what and fell face first. (I have a habit of tripping on air.) I lay on the floor of the stage with my dress up, the cameras rolling and my children in the front row. I felt a silence descend in the large hall. I wanted to stay down, not get up. (Could I just disappear into the ground?)

Someone helped me up, and I felt my face grow hot and red with embarrassment. I pulled my dress down and straightened myself out. It was everyone's worst nightmare. I had made a complete fool of myself. Everyone asked me if I was alright, even late into the evening. I just wanted to curl myself into a ball but, instead, I learned to laugh at myself that night. My boys made jokes about my fall after they knew I was OK.

Naturally shy, I was never a public speaker. My nerves would get the best of me, my voice shook, and my hands trembled with sweat. After experiencing the worst possible scenario, how could I be scared to speak in public? This embarrassing incident gave me the courage at public forums to promote early education in my county. I began public speaking shortly after.

As a natural progression of my work with children, I became involved in politics when I realized that some legislation directly affected them. The state budget could easily cut funds for subsidy care, and the health care of children was impacted when state services were altered by legislation. Local childcare providers and I traveled to the state capitol for "Action Day" to speak with our politicians about the importance of keeping children in mind when budget cuts were considered.

In order to reach more local politicians, I set up an "Early Care and Education Forum" at my local library. I invited state representatives, state senators, and county commissioners to a bipartisan panel to acknowledge and discuss the importance of early care and education. I single-handedly organized and coordinated events, and even enticed the media to cover these often-overlooked gatherings to spread the word regarding early childcare and education. I was an advocate for high-quality childcare for all children. I demonstrated that family childcare is more than just a babysitting service.

I also invited the same politicians to my program for story time and snacks. I gave them tours of my small childcare (that I was very proud of). They would read books to the class, and then they joined the children for healthy snacks. I regarded politicians as regular people. They were approachable, and I could express my concerns to them. By giving them an inside look at my childcare, I opened their eyes to the value of my work and the necessity of quality childcare programs in our area.

A couple years later, I was invited to the Terri Lynn Lokoff Child Care Foundation Awards to talk to the new winners regarding my advocacy work. I began my speech with the following remark: "I remember being scared of public speaking, but once you fall down wearing a dress in front of cameras on live TV, nothing worse or more embarrassing can happen." I hold that embarrassing moment in my mind whenever I give a speech or offer training. Just in case, though, I make sure my outfits cannot have wardrobe malfunctions. And I wear shorter heels.

The local AEYC board submitted my name to the Pennsylvania Child Care Association (PACCA) for their Educator of the Year award. As the first and only family childcare provider in my county to be accredited, and because of my advocacy work, the awards committee felt I deserved the 2007 award. My work was valued. I felt honored, and my voice cracked when I gave my acceptance speech. And I did not trip on stage!

I also worked with the Pocono Healthy Communities Alliance on a committee to demonstrate to the public the learning-through-play method. We set up demonstrations in our local mall during April's "Week of the Young Child," and local childcare centers joined us for the day. Families and kids from around the county played different games and learned about quality early-childhood education. We also created brochures about quality early care and education.

I continued to use my experience to teach in other areas. East Stroudsburg University and Northampton Community College asked me for permission to send their students who were seeking early education degrees to my childcare for internships. I accepted these students because I loved teaching others how to properly run a worthwhile childcare. In due course, I was filmed teaching math and science to children using songs and rhymes. My work was used in a course (Earl 201: Teaching Math and Science with Mixed Ages) at Northampton Community College.

In 2008, I was awarded the NAFCC Individual Leadership award through High Reach learning. I was flown to California to the NAFCC National Conference. This was the first time in nine years that I was by myself—no kids or husband. It was a nice respite. It also was the first time I attended a NAFCC conference. I was overwhelmed by the number of teachers and educators gathered. In the opening keynote, I looked around the grand ballroom and realized the people in that huge room were mainly educators or providers, just like me. I finally got to meet people whose values were similar to mine and who truly loved their work. I met some great people in this field. One afternoon, a group of us decided to walk around Disneyland together after being in the conference all day. I networked, and it felt great connecting with other childcare professionals. At the awards dinner, I was presented with an incredible award. I learned so much at this wonderful conference. I came back energized and with many ideas to implement with my class.

My work was fun. It was something I truly enjoyed, and I looked forward to every day. I had found my niche in life, and I loved it. I was using music daily to extend learning with the children too. When I started back in 1999, I never thought my success could be possible. I had known so little and thought childcare was easy. It was far from it, but hard work and education paid off. My success was the embodiment of these tenets. I was not a babysitter.

Stroudsburg day care earns national recognition again

Monroe County's only nationally accredited family-based child care center had its status reauthorized last month.

Angela's Child Development is run out of the Stroudsburg home of Angela Bayer. It was accredited on Nov. 15 for three more years by the National Association for Family Child Care, which advocates for and accredits family-based child care centers. There are 49 nationally accredited family-based centers in the state and nearly 2,000 nationwide.

The association recently boosted its criteria, as did the National Association for the Education of Young Children, which fulfills a similar purpose for center-based child care providers.

Bayer had to submit to a nearly 11-month process of evaluations, observations and self-assessment. She had to meet goals related to curriculum, teaching, child assessment, health, community relationships and other areas.

But she embraced the challenge. "It's great because it actually ups the quality of child care," Bayer said of the standards. "When parents come here, they say they're dropping their kids off at school. It's not baby-sitting."

Angela's Child Development was first accredited in 2004. It serves six children full-time and one part-time. "It's more of a family," she said. "That's what I like about this."

In recent years, Bayer has earned a Child Development Associate Credential from the Council for Professional Recognition in Washington, D.C.; the Individual Leadership Award from the National Association of Family Child Care and High Reach Learning; and the Terri Lynn Lokoff Child Care Foundation National Child Care Teacher Award from Tylenol, which brought her and her center $1,000 in prize money.

—Dan Berrett

MONDAY
October 27, 2008

Forum promotes early education efforts

By ADAM McNAUGHTON
Pocono Record Writer

STROUDSBURG — State representatives from Monroe County and local advocates for early childhood education agreed on Sunday that preparing children to enter school should be a priority — but finding state funds will always be difficult.

"It is an impossibility for those of us in Harrisburg to reconcile the desire of some to reduce taxes with the desire of others to increase funding for worthy programs and that is the central challenge," said Mike Carroll, D-118.

Carroll spoke at a forum Sunday at Hughes Library in Stroudsburg for local representatives to discuss early educa-

tion issues with area educators and caregivers.

State Reps. Mario Scavello, R-176, and John Siptroth, D-189, also attended the event — discussing early education issues and answering questions from some of the 35 people at the forum.

"The best investment we can make in our children is at a very

young age so when they are getting to first grade they are ready and ready to go," Scavello said.

But increased investment for education — and anything else — will likely be hurt, Scavello said. He called this year's budgets one of the most difficult the state has faced, saying the state currently has an approximately

See **FORUM**, Page A2

FORUM

From Page **A1**

$280 million budget shortfall and could face a $2.5 billion deficit for the year.

Besides securing state funding for programs like Head Start, questions from the audi-

ence focuses on increasing parent participation in children's education and programs for special needs students.

Angela Bayer, and early childhood care provider, helped organize the event and acted as a moderator — asking the three representatives questions and taking questions from the audience. She called early childhood

education an investment that creates better students once they enter school, saving money on special education.

"We need to give every parent the chance to place their child, if they want, in a quality early care and education program that helps their child grow and develop to the best of their abilities," Bayer said.

Stroud Twp. child care pro gets state award

HARRISBURG — Angela Bayer of Stroud Township was recently presented with the annual Educator of the Year award by the Pennsylvania Child Care Association. This award acknowledges outstanding direct care and education of young children.

Bayer's colleagues at Angela's Child Development described her as committed. "She brings community leaders such as county commissioners, state representatives, and other professionals, including firefighters and wildlife conservation workers, into the classroom," one coworker said. Bayer is also known for community involvement. Her fellow-educators say that she makes others a part of her work by advocating through workshops, public speaking at county and state meetings, and by working with her local community.

Bayer, a mother of three, a step-mother of four, and a grandmother of two, believes that quality child care begins with understanding and love. "I have to agree with John Lennon when he sings, 'all we need is love.' Children need love to thrive and prosper."

Bayer had this to say of her job, "Every day is a new challenge in child care and every day should begin with a smile to a child when they walk in through the door. ...I am here to be their 'day mom.' I am here to understand their quirks and fears. But most of all, I am here to help them grow and be the best possible person that they can be."

The honor was presented for the first time in a special awards ceremony during the statewide Early Childhood Education Summit in State College in October.

Pennsylvania Child Care Association is a state-wide nonprofit 501(c)3 organization whose mission is to facilitate the provision of quality early care and education to the children of Pennsylvania. Its members provide care to over 200,000 children in the Commonwealth from infants through school age. For more information, visit www.pacca.org.

C 2 Wednesday, September 5, 2007

Child care provider wins national award

A local family child care provider has won a national award for her work.

Angela Bayer, owner and operator of Angela's Child Development in Bartonsville, won the Individual Leadership Award from the National Association of Family Child Care and High Reach Learning.

The National Association Family Child Care is a national membership organization that accredits family child care providers. High Reach Learning is a company that creates educational books, toys and games for children between 3 months and 14 years old.

Angela Bayer

Bayer was the sole winner of the national award. She was selected for her work in carrying out the association's mission for the family child care field. Other criteria included demonstrating leadership through mentoring, advocacy, community outreach and professional development.

As winner of the award, Bayer will receive $500 in High Reach Learning products and services, round-trip airfare and a two-night stay in Anaheim, Calif. for the association's annual conference this year.

Bayer is Monroe County's only family care provider who has been accredited for the last four years by the association. She is also four-star rated in the Keystone Star program, a measure of quality established by the state.

Last year, she won the Terri Lynn Lokoff Child Care Foundation National Child Care Teacher Award from Tylenol, which brought her and her center $1,000 in prize money.

Bayer is looking into future plans of creating quality preschool program open for more children in Luzerne, Lackawanna and Monroe counties.

10

BEHIND THE SCENES

MY STORY COULD FINISH HERE on a happy note (and very short book), and I hesitate to continue. This section offers the part of my life I kept quiet. No clients, neighbors, friends, or even family had been privy to my private life because I managed to keep my private and public lives separate. However, my professional and personal lives clashed in July 2010.

As I explained earlier, family childcare providers have a unique situation because they use their homes as businesses. Families merge their lives with the childcares. In my case, my situation looked great— even perfect. I lived in a beautiful, brand-new, 4,500-square-foot house. It was the porch-with-rocking-chairs house—the one most people in the country dream of owning.

The sad truth was my marriage was far from a fairy tale. I felt trapped. My husband was not an easy person to live with by any stretch of the imagination. He appeared in public as a caring and loving man. My extended family had no idea what was going on behind closed doors. My husband was careful to act in a certain acceptable way in public. Only immediate family knew how he really behaved.

My husband became a public figure, speaking up for children's rights and against child abuse. He undertook this advocacy role when we discovered through our own dealings with Children and Youth Services, that Pennsylvania had no ombudsman. The incident took place in 2004. Gabriel (12) and Peter (10) returned from a weekend with their father, my ex-husband, acting very weird. Peter looked sick and lethargic. I took him to the emergency room and discovered he was drunk. Peter had taken sips from open alcohol containers at a family party while with his father. No one realized he was drinking alcohol. No blame here. It could have happened to anyone and anywhere.

The doctors at the ER reported this incident to Children and Youth services as required by law. We were called and required to visit the Children and Youth office with the boys. At this time, we were served a notice that the boys were going into foster care because the authorities needed to investigate the case. I was shocked. How could they take my sons? How could they keep them? This only happens to drug dealers or child abusers, I thought. How and why did this happen to my family? Those questions were never answered. I was forced to leave the Children and Youth office without my boys as they screamed for me. I was physically pulled away from my boys. My boys were held back by caseworkers as they screamed and ran for me. I could not believe this was happening.

No officer ever served us a protection order or any order, as required by law. (We were not familiar with this law at the time.) Six days later, we attended a court hearing. (By law, a hearing should be held in three days. Little did we know.) I was told a psychologist needed to speak with my boys without any coaching or parental influence, and the boys had to stay in foster care until the evaluations were completed. I was in shock. I do not know how I functioned during this time. My life was my children, and now my two older boys were ripped from me. Their father had no idea how to fight Children and Youth services either. We each got our own lawyers to try to fight and get the boys back home.

We were told we could not have any contact with our boys during their foster care. This was foreign to me. No contact. I had no idea what my boys were doing, what they were eating, how they were feeling, where they were sleeping, who they were with. I was a zombie without Gabriel or Peter. I cried in their beds at night. I smelled their pillows and wanted to keep their scent close to me. I needed my substitute to work with me during the day with the class because I could barely function.

During that time, I discovered the judge's daughter and the county lawyer's son were in Gabriel's class at a small private school with only 21 students per grade. We all knew each other; it's a very small community. Gabriel's best friend was in the same class. His father, who was the local reporter, learned about and wanted to write about our story. It was big news that my children had been taken from me without a proper warrant and, meanwhile, I was caring for other people's children. It made no sense.

My childcare business was not impacted by the dire circumstances. No investigation of me or my husband took place. But I wondered why the psychologist didn't meet the boys while they lived at home. I questioned the agency daily. I called constantly. Calls were not returned. I would go to the office and was told to go home. I was frantic to get my boys home. The boys were moved seven times to different foster homes. This was a small town, and everyone knew what was going on. They recognized the boys. Foster parents did not want to get involved with the boys because they did not want any public backlash. One foster parent later told me she could not walk out of her house without her neighbors yelling at her to return my boys.

My clients were upset for me. I kept them informed every step of the way. No one could comprehend why if there was no investigation on me, why then were my own boys removed from their home. It made no sense. The county solicitor refused to speak to us. At one point, one caseworker admitted she was trying to correct things as quickly as possible, but her hands were tied. The case was in the court's hands. (Several caseworkers had no idea I ran a childcare. The irony was not lost on anyone.)

While the boys were in the foster-care system, I reached out to anyone who could help me. I started with local politicians, state legislators, and county commissioners. I was desperate for my boys. I even called the White House. I do not recall how I got the number. (When I called, I was told to never call that number again! I think I had accidentally dialed a private number.)

On Feb. 20, 2014, I returned to court to get my boys back. I was told by the reporter that he heard through the grapevine the case might be continued, so he was going to write another story to put pressure on the court to release my sons. The court wanted to keep the boys longer because the boys' "language was too advanced for their ages." It was believed that they could have been coached into stating what happened. The boys were saying that they just drank from open cups, but no adult present knew they had or was informed of what they did.

Obviously, they had advanced language. They read—all the time. Their grasp of English was extensive. The reporter asked the county solicitor and psychologist for interviews. They replied, "No comment."

The reporter's presence made a difference in court. The power of the press added pressure to an already heated and debated local topic. The court was made aware that a story would be written. When I walked into court, the judge told me before the proceedings started that the boys were coming home that day. I couldn't believe it. Finally. The case was not going to be continued. The nightmare was going to be over. Our case was unfounded. No adults were held responsible, rightfully so. There would be no follow-ups with the court or caseworkers.

When the boys came out from a back room, I threw my arms around them, and we fell to the floor, and I just cried. They cried. I cradled and rocked them in my arms, while on my knees with my arms around both of them. We stayed in that position for a long time, ignoring everyone around us. I was not letting anyone take them again. It had been 41 days of hell. I learned the hard way the system was flawed. *Individual cases must be reviewed, and blanket rules cannot be applied to everyone.*

After this incident, we became well-recognized in town by the county commissioners, state senators. They came over to my house for coffee and tea. We lived very public lives. We held rallies to speak up for children. We discovered there was no state ombudsman, so I joined a board to help write a provisional bill for the state House of Representatives. Child molestation was not a felony in Pennsylvania and, as a family, we wrote a petition and gathered more than 150,000 names supporting the bill. I needed something good to come out of suffering those 41 days. I needed to further this purpose. We worked together to make a difference in our community and state.

Our lives were always under a microscope. At home, after the child-care children went home, things were different, though. My husband became a belligerent, manipulative and angry person. I confided in my sister-in-law after she got a hint something was up with us. She let me cry on her shoulder when he acted manipulative and hurtful. She tried to open my eyes to what his cries for help were—manipulations. My husband had many health issues, and I hired a nurse to help take care of him during my workday. She became a member of the household. My husband took several heart and blood-pressure medications. He required attention I could not give him because I was working.

One day, I took my boys to Knoebels Amusement Resort. Before we barely traveled two miles, my husband called me to demand that

I return home. I asked why. He said he needed me at home to care for him; he did not like me going out without him. If I did not come home, he threatened, no, he promised, he would release all our pets into the wild. The boys cried because they knew he meant it, and now we could not go to the amusement park. This is just one example of how he manipulated us.

My oldest two boys were now teenagers, and they were not easy, like most teenagers. Unfortunately, my husband magnified family issues by disrespecting them or treating them too harshly. My oldest son Gabriel loved soccer. My husband punished him when he left his shoes out of the shoe cubbies. By punished, I mean he screamed in his face for "making a mess" in his living room. He would ground him and take away his soccer privileges for two-to-four weeks—all this punishment for shoes left out of the cubby. When I tried to intercede on my son's behalf, I got yelled at to my face; we were nose to nose. I had to back up. This was one incident of many. We were never on the same page regarding the raising of my boys.

My husband said I could not treat the boys like my childcare children. He did not approve of my respectful teaching. He wanted to make my boys respect him. I believe respect is taught by example and earned through actions. He laughed at this idea. He thought the way I talked to children was wrong. He talked down to my boys, not with them. I treated children with respect and earned it back. Daily, continuous, hurtful situations happened.

My second oldest son Peter bore the brunt of my husband's anger. My husband sneered and ridiculed him continually. I was proud of his schoolwork, yet when Peter achieved a C on an exam, my husband snarled and said, "What? You can't get an A?" No grade was good enough for him. I was proud of a C from Peter. It meant he had worked hard for it. Not everyone's best effort is an A. When I told Peter I thought he made a good effort, my husband laughed and scoffed that Peter's grade was not good enough and he did not deserve praise for mediocre work.

* * *

Angela's Advice

Every child's A or best effort is different. Everyone excels at different things and learns differently.

TALKING BACK WAS TREATED as a felony. My husband did not want anyone, much less a child, contradicting him. One day, Peter talked back to him and refused to clean his room. For that, my husband forced him to rake leaves—in the woods! Leaves belong in the woods. It was an inane punishment. His brother's birthday party was taking place at this time. Peter was not allowed into the house until the raking was done. My parents, who were over for the party, were livid, and so was I. My husband had declared Peter's punishment during the party. I tried not to make a scene, but I wanted Peter at the party with the family. Consequently, I argued with my husband about his needless, idiotic punishment. He growled at me to watch myself and to not undermine him—ever. I asked Peter to come in, and my husband locked himself in his bedroom for the rest of the weekend. I made excuses for him to my family, telling them he was not feeling well. He didn't speak to me for a month after that. He threatened to commit suicide and was blaming me for being a horrible wife. He made me feel responsible for his moods and his actions. Life was slowly falling apart.

Another unpleasant memory is how the boys' Halloween candy was always confiscated after we returned from trick or treating. My husband said sugar was bad for the boys, and he would take the whole stash after they went to bed. He would eat it. In the following days, when they asked for it back, he'd refuse. So, they would sneak into his room to take it back and got into more trouble for "stealing candy." This hoarding of the children's candy was an annual occurrence. It got to a point when the boys did not want to go trick or treating. Why bother? They could go to the gas station and buy candy instead.

John, my third oldest son, escaped every day. He would go climb the trees to do his homework. I would check to see if his shoes were missing to know whether he had gone outside. His father called on him constantly to deliver a Diet Coke, bring him his pills, help to put on his shoes and on and on. John observed everything and stayed out of everyone's way. He learned early in life to stay away from his father when he got in one of his moods. His solution was to go to the woods.

Another instance took place during a bad winter snowstorm. (Snowfalls in Pennsylvania were measured by feet, not inches.) I bought a snowblower, but, unfortunately, it did not come assembled. I needed to build it myself because my husband was not physically able to help. I found out—neither am I. I *thought* I put it together correctly. It looked right. It turned on fine. During the first heavy snowfall, I started the machine. I took a couple of steps and heard something hit the side of the house. The screws went flying off the snowblower, and one struck the window, breaking it. I had not tightened the screws well. My husband came outside screaming. He thought the boys had thrown a snowball at the window. He did not let me explain. He shrieked so much they cried. When he finally heard me, he did not apologize for shouting. He switched to hollering at me for breaking *his* window and for not knowing how to assemble a snowblower. My husband hit me with his words. My spirit broke under his rule.

I tried to stand up to my husband, remarking how his punitive ways were negatively impacting the boys. We would talk, and it would seem as if things would change for a week or two, but they never did. His broken promises broke my heart. Broken hearts are like a plate shattered on the floor. It could be put back together with glue, but it is never whole again.

Walking in with muddy shoes, dirty laundry in their rooms, remote control not left by the TV—these were all reasons my husband threatened and screamed and grounded the boys from their fun activities. As an ex-marine, he expected the boys to abide by a certain militaristic standard. When I spoke up, he sneered and belittled me. "This is my house, my rules," he said.

Before we met, my husband built the house with money from a settlement. It was his floor plan, his idea, his dreamhouse. He wound up taking out a mortgage on it to buy furniture, pay landscapers and buy cars for his ex-wife and kids. (His ex-wife and kids had left him. They had taken everything with them, and he was left with the mortgage payments.) When I met him, he was unable to pay the mortgage, and my job as a caseworker paid the bills. Later, my childcare business paid the mortgage and taxes and bills of the house. He lived off his Social Security checks.

When we first got together, he told me my name would be added to the house's deed. He made a point of telling my parents the house was also mine. I believed him. I was naive enough to trust him and not ask for proof. I was never added to the mortgage or to the deed. I could not speak to the mortgage company without his consent, according to the law. I became aware of this rule when our taxes increased, and I had to contact the mortgage company to add a payment. When I questioned my husband about it, he dismissed me. Years later, he admitted to me in anger that he had never planned on adding my name. I felt like the rug was pulled out from under me.

Security was something I needed for me and my boys. Once I knew the house was only his, my husband made a point of expressing, "this is my house." My boys also understood this house was not their house and, as such, not their home. We were guests in my husband's house. Consequently, life was in limbo during my husband's bad moods and his threats were ominous. We lived in tension. I had a smile on my face during the day with the children in my care. I had to wear my mask. After work hours, I was free to take off my mask.

Gabriel could not live like this anymore. He ran away to his best friend's house. There he spent the month watching the 2010 World Cup and enjoying his freedom. I could not get him to come back home. We met at Dunkin' Donuts and had a true heart-to-heart. Gabriel wanted things to change at home. He preferred to be home with his family, but could not live with the pressure, stress, screaming, humiliation and degradation anymore. I told him I would stick up for him more. I needed to be a stronger mother to him and all my sons. I assured him that I would defend them, but we both knew it was my husband who needed to change. I told Gabriel I would talk to my husband and help him change his abhorrent behavior. Gabe came back home.

11

JULY 2010

I T WAS THE SUMMER OF 2010, and my second oldest Peter was visiting a friend in New York, and my youngest John was away at summer camp. I was home for the Fourth of July weekend with my oldest son Gabriel and husband. My husband was in his mood—the mood that caused me to walk on eggshells because he could easily be set off. My neck was stressed and painful from the tension.

My husband found a glass in the living room—used glassware in the living room. That minor mistake was enough kindling to ignite a fury inside my husband. He screamed at my son. Gabriel stood up to him and yelled back. He was no longer a child. He was 17. It was just a dirty glass that he was going to pick up, and there was no need for the drama. I stepped in for my son and got shouted at, spit flying at my face. He called my oldest a "slob" and "disrespectful" for messing up his living room. I asked him to calm down, knowing full well that once my husband got like this, there was no turning back. He hollered at me: "You are my wife! You need to follow my rules!" I stepped back as he stepped toward me. He had never escalated his anger to outright violence, but he backed me into the wall. He screamed, "Wife comes before mother!" I argued and continued to stand up for my son. "You can't defy me. I'm the number one in this house, not your sons," he bellowed.

Gabe couldn't deal with my husband anymore. This was more than he could handle. He asked to go to a friend's house for the weekend. I thought he deserved to have some fun for the Fourth of July, so I told him to go. My husband demanded he stay, but I blocked him. If Gabe wanted to go, he could go. Gabe left. This made my husband angrier. He went to the den and threw items around. He broke porcelain statues and tossed books around. I glanced at the room and backed away. It looked like we had been robbed. Everything was dumped and damaged. Then he screamed that he was going to kick me out. I knew it was going to be a long weekend.

Throughout the years, my husband made me feel that I could not function without him. He had ingrained in me over time that I was incapable of surviving without him. My business was in his house. He called it *his* business, although he never did anything to help. He came downstairs after work hours. My sister-in-law noted her brother was emotionally abusive toward me, but I could not believe her. I was a mother and professional. I had worked as a volunteer for Women's Resources, an agency that helps women and children in abusive situations. I did not think that I had put myself in a position to be abused. Looking back, though, I was a shell of myself. I did not know who I was. During 12 years with this man, he conditioned me to accept his anger and moods to the point that I considered them normal. I believed I had no choice but to accept my husband's foul moods. He was my husband, after all, and we had married in the Catholic Church. That meant something to me.

Later that night in bed, I stayed on my side of the bed, careful not to upset him further by moving or making noises. Past experiences had taught me when he was in this loathsome mood, I needed to be quiet, and he would calm down on his own. Noises, no matter how soft, would reignite his volatile temper. He was even angrier than usual because I had stood up for my son and had allowed him to leave for the weekend.

In the middle of the night, as I lay on my side facing the wall, I felt his arms around my chest. At first, I thought he was trying to hug me to make up. He usually did this after his angry bouts. That was the cycle of abuse he had weaved. But this time, he started hugging harder. So hard. All of a sudden, I felt a sharp stabbing pain. I found it hard to breathe. His arms were like vise grips around my chest. I could not move. It hurt to breathe or talk. I could not scream. His grip grew tighter around my chest.

My breathing was growing shallow and I felt light-headed. Abruptly, he let go. He watched me taking slow breaths and asked, "What the hell is your problem?" I whispered to him that he had hurt me. I could barely talk. He glared at me and demanded that I stop playacting. He told me he had been asleep.

I did not know what to believe other than the undeniable pain in my chest. He turned around and went to sleep, and I tried, without success, to get comfortable. I lay in bed the rest of the night, aching and not knowing what to think. When the sun rose, I realized I could barely move. I had to get to the hospital. I drove myself to the hospital, and he tagged along. He said he needed to make sure I was OK. Driving was painful and, when I made the first turn, I realized I could not breathe. I felt a stabbing pain in my chest. He took over driving.

We arrived at Pocono Medical Center early in the morning on July 4, 2010. After X-rays, I learned I had three broken ribs. Three broken ribs. The doctor asked what happened, and my husband answered, "I just hugged her too hard!" The doctor was familiar with us because my husband had visited him several times for his many health issues. No one questioned what led to my broken ribs. No one spoke to me privately or asked me if I was safe. In the bathroom, I saw signs advising women what to do in an abusive relationship. I knew what to do in abusive situations. The hospital report disclosed that no one spoke to me in private or asked if I was safe. I wondered how many other women have left a hospital like I did that day.

But what could I do anyway? I was with him in the hospital every minute, except when I went to the bathroom, and who would believe me? Everyone knew my husband, including the doctors and nurses.

Honestly, I did not want anyone to know. This was embarrassing. I was embarrassed. Meanwhile, he walked around very confidently with a smile on his face. I was badly injured and would need to rely on him. I tried my best to keep up appearances at the hospital, but the charade had collapsed around me. I just did not know it yet.

When we got home, I stayed in bed the rest of the day and used pillows to keep my body in a somewhat comfortable position. My husband was attentive and sweet to me, offering to bring up my meals. When Gabriel called, he told my son I was resting for the day. My husband's sister called, as well. She heard in my voice that something was wrong. I told her what happened. Our conversation helped open my eyes. While I talked with her, I realized what was really going on. I was finally voicing my fears. It felt like a fog had lifted. She advised me to call the cops and get him out of the house before he did something worse—now! Her advice made me wonder whether he *could* do something more. What if he tried? I could not protect myself. I could barely move.

Everything my sister-in-law said made sense, and my heart knew this. She voiced my fears out loud. But I was scared to seek help. I had been conditioned into doubting myself. Through the years, my husband had effectively molded me into someone I did not recognize. I was a shadow of a woman. I had no friends. Literally. I never called or talked to anyone, other than colleagues or clients. I did not want to confide in them now. Slowly, throughout the years, I had lost all contact with everyone. He had monopolized my time and demanded I, as his wife, needed to be there for *him*. He had made it impossible to continue any friendships because I could not have phone contact or meet with anyone. I could not remember the last time I had a nice long talk on the phone, and I never participated in a girls' night out.

I wondered if anyone would believe me? How would I be safe? I feared the repercussions. What if I spoke up and no one believed me, and then he got even angrier with me? I needed protection. I was familiar with the abuse-reporting process, but the difficult step was getting past the emotional part.

* * *

Angela's Advice

If you or anyone you know is a victim of abuse, keep in mind the hardest step is not contacting authorities or reporting the abuse— it is the getting over the emotional hurdle of acknowledging the abuse. Support systems for those abused are hard to find, but they are there. Doctors and nurses can help.

* * *

WHEN I VOLUNTEERED with women in domestic violence, I never fully understood how hard it was to fight back. Now, ironically, I was in the same position myself. I could not bring myself to pursue help, even now. Maybe my chance had passed when I walked out of the hospital with him and returned home. Who would believe a man like him could do this to a woman like me? Wouldn't they wonder why I had come home with him, not understanding that I felt like I had no choice? From my experience, I knew domestic violence had no racial, ethical, sexual orientation or socioeconomic divides. Anyone could be affected by it. But still, me?

I could not call my parents. In the past, they had proved to be unreliable. In the worst time of my life, before my second husband, I had found myself in a horrible position. With half a tank of gas in an old car and no cash or credit cards, I vividly remember calling my mother collect from a payphone and asking her for help. She said, "You made your bed, now lay in it." And she hung up the phone. I couldn't call my father either because his hearing loss made phone calls impossible.

Unfortunately, my mother and I did not speak to each other for years after that phone call. I lived in my car for several nights. Luckily, it was summer, so the temperature was okay. I lived in a shelter for several months after that. I slowly got back on my feet—on my own. Based on that experience years ago, I could not call her now and have my mom tell me the same thing. I could not deal with her rejection.

My husband's emotional abuse had crossed the line into physical for the first time. I needed to protect myself. Gabriel was at a friend's house for the night and I was alone with my husband. Somewhere, deep inside me, I found some strength to know what to do. Somehow, I wobbled out of bed and locked the bedroom door while he was downstairs in the kitchen. I placed a chair in front of the door like I had seen in a movie. I regarded the door. Should I unlock it before he figured it out? Was I losing my nerve? I paused. Then I walked back to bed, trembling. I carefully laid down and shivered—not from cold, but from fear.

When he came back upstairs, he discovered the locked door. This act was complete defiance in his eyes. There was no turning back as far as I was concerned. He pounded on the door, then thrust himself against it. The hinges loosened. I was terrified. He bellowed at me to open the door or else "you'll find out what I'm made of." I was alone in the bedroom with only him in the house. "This is my house, my bedroom. You can't lock me out."

Even if I screamed, neighbors would not hear me. The houses in our neighborhood were widely spaced. After what felt like hours, but was only minutes, he stopped. He walked away for a bit, then walked back and banged on the door again. Next, he begged me to open the door because he had food for me.

I threatened to call the cops. He laughed. His laugh was one I remember well—maniacal. My hands shook as I picked up the phone to call 911—no dial tone. I stared at the phone, realizing the main phone line was hooked into his office. He must have unplugged it. I searched for my cell phone until I remembered I had left it in my purse in the foyer—worst timing for my bad habit of losing my phone. I had locked myself in the bedroom with no way to call for help. Climbing out the second-story window with three broken ribs was not an option. All I could do was hope and pray that he could not break down the door.

I do not know why he gave up. Was he tired, or had he realized I was securely locked inside? I could not leave—bad planning on my part or rather, no planning.

All was silent for a while. He must have gone downstairs or to his den. I rested as much as I could, propped up in bed. Broken ribs were no joke. Every breath hurt. Every move was painful. I did not sleep all night, worried that he would figure out a way in. My fear paralyzed me. I needed to get past my fear of him and get myself out of this jam.

Tuesday morning, with the sun showing me the light of day, I rose and changed clothes as quickly as I could. With broken ribs, lifting my arms to put on my shirt was painful. Bending hurt. I grabbed my hair into a bun and threw on a baseball cap. There was no way I could make my hair look decent because brushing my frizzy hair was difficult with my injury.

I walked downstairs quietly and, from the foyer, I heard him snoring on the living-room couch. Thankfully, I did not have to see him. I went to my files and snatched the folder with the childcare emergency numbers. Then, I grabbed my purse and walked out of the house. I drove to a nearby gas station and notified my client families the childcare was closed for the day because of an emergency. The calls with the clients were short because I did not want to lose my momentum or get upset on the phone. Also, there was no need to go into details at this time about what had happened.

Luckily, my childcare contract stipulated that I could take personal days, and it required parents to have back-up childcare available if I had an emergency. I hated using this clause, but I had no choice. My substitute would replace me for the next several weeks because of my broken ribs. Next, I drove carefully down to the courthouse. Driving was difficult, especially parallel parking.

I knew what I had to do. I had helped many other women in my circumstances. I just never imagined I would be the one asking a judge for a Protection from Abuse order (PFA).

The guards greeted me. Many of them knew me from my advocacy work. This task was going to be harder than I thought because I could not do it anonymously. I explained to the guards I was headed to the prothonotary's office. "Oh, good luck, hope it works out for them."

The guards thought I was there to help someone else.

My situation had me deliberating about the different masks we wear in public. People knew me. But really, how many of us really know each other? All of us have our demons we effectively hide from the public. We have our private lives. We wear our masks in public. My mask was coming off. I would be stripped naked in public. My story would be on public record.

I walked into the prothonotary's office and asked for a PFA request form. With a shaky, nervous hand, I wrote the events of the last 72 hours on the form. I signed the paper, hands still trembling. And I cried. Not soft cries no one notices. I am talking 'hurt-my-ribs, need- air sobs.' My marriage was over. It had been over for a long time, but I had not realized it until that moment. My facade was down. This piece of paper requesting a PFA sealed the end of my marriage. I was ashamed of myself.

This was the first and only time I shed tears for my marriage. The crying was cathartic. I had the strength to move forward into the unknown. The clerk advised me that a temporary PFA had been granted. I needed to return to court in a few days to have a judge hear my case. This temporary order allowed me to have my husband removed from the house. At the sheriff's office, they told me my husband would be escorted out of the house later that same day.

When I returned home, I found that my husband had locked himself in the bedroom. It was a relief because I could hear him if he came out. His nurse, Stan, told me he had been demanding to go to the bank and wondered about my whereabouts. She had reminded him that he had a doctor's appointment, and he refused to go. This behavior was his norm. He skipped doctor's appointments continuously. He purposely would not take his medications to make himself sicker, so he could wind up in the hospital. He manipulated us with his ill health.

Life with this man revolved around his moods. I could not be manipulated anymore. I told his nurse what was going on, and she gave me a gentle hug. Stan assured me that filing the PFA was the best thing I could have done. She wished me the best.

Stan reminded me that my husband had ranted to her about cleaning out our joint bank account. Our savings had been depleted in May when the septic tank blew and we installed a new one, plus we remodeled one bathroom and had the landscaping redone around the septic tank. During the renovations, we had lived at the local Howard Johnson's. That month had been extremely costly. The several thousand dollars left in the account was not much, but it was my hard-earned money. My husband relied on disability as his sole income.

I made it a point of going to the bank that afternoon to take out my money. I left his Social Security deposits. I did not close the account because he received his checks directly deposited. I did open up another account in my name only. I needed to be able to pay bills. After I explained the situation to Gabriel, he, gently, because of my broken ribs, gave me a big hug. "It's going to be okay, Mom." But would it?

Shortly after I arrived home from the bank, three officers from the sheriff's department came to escort my unknowing husband out of his house. When they knocked on his bedroom door, he thought it was me and screamed to get away. When he realized it was the sheriff's men, he could not have been more surprised. He was incredulous that I had gone to such lengths to remove him, and he became violent. He had to be restrained by the men while he was walked out to keep from harming me. He lunged once at me, and they held him back. "This is *my* house. You can't make me leave!" The look he gave me cut to my core. It was pure hatred and loathing. He was instructed not to have phone, physical, or any third-party contact with me. The sheriff's officers were adamant about the rules, and they reiterated the rules of the PFA. Any contact would mean immediate jail time. Then, the officials drove him to the local Howard Johnson hotel. He would be staying less than a mile away.

While he was driven away, I stared at the taillights on the sheriff's car. I was in a daze. I had no idea what would happen when we went to court the following Monday, but, for now, I had a week of freedom.

I called my sister-in-law with the news. She said this was all for the best. She listened to me and was very attentive to me. She encouraged me not to fall for any more manipulations and to stay strong. She reminded me I was the only reason that either one of his sisters talked to him. Prior to getting together with me, my husband's sisters and their families did not interact with him. I believed my husband when he declared it was their fault. He tried to convince me that his sisters had wronged him in some way. In reality, they knew how he manipulated and emotionally hurt people. Consequently, they did not remain in contact with him. I had managed, throughout our 12 years, to bring them back together. When it was over between us, neither sister ever spoke to him again.

I said my goodbye to my husband's nurse, Stan. She had been a friend to me. "Be strong. You know what you're doing. You know what needs to be done," she said. Stan was a no-nonsense woman. I loved that about her. She was someone I needed to be more like in the future. I needed to speak up for myself and love myself again. But first, I needed to discover who I was. I had been conditioned and manipulated for so long, I did not recognize myself anymore.

Gabriel and I ordered Chinese food for dinner that night. We ate, watched television and even left our cups in the living room. No one yelled at us for the mess, which felt strange. The house had an eerie feel to it. It was like the tension built up from many years had no place to go. It was hollow, empty.

In my bedroom that night, the first thing I did with Gabriel's help was change the sheets, then I lit some aromatic candles. I wanted a new scent and feel to the room. Gabe moved my husband's pillows and blankets off the bed and stored them away. Gabriel also vacuumed and cleaned up the disaster in the den my husband created—tedious work.

The bathroom and bedroom smelled fresh, and the bedroom had a different aura about it. Nothing but the pillows and a blanket had been moved, but, still, that was enough. The aromatic candle seemed to add peace to the room. I felt safe. For the first time in three days, I felt like I could sleep. For the first time in too many years, I felt comfortable in the bedroom. The future was going to be challenging. I had a lot of decisions to make and a lot to consider. But there was no going back.

The next day, my other two sons were coming home. We would have a hard conversation about what had happened—startling news for them. Yet, I doubted they would be upset. Peter had been in the city and saw museums and went to movies. He was excited and happy to tell me about his adventures in New York with his friends.

When Peter entered the house, he immediately noticed my husband's shoes were missing, but the car was there. I sat him down and gave him as much necessary information as I thought a 16-year-old could grasp. Peter looked blankly at me. "He's gone? He's gone?" The relief on this child's face was incredible. He leaned back and relaxed on the couch.

John was only 11, and this man was his father, so I thought this news would be difficult for him to handle. We all had protected him from his father's anger. I remember hiding him in a closet one night so his father would not yell at him during a rampage about a broken faucet. When I told John, he responded with a practical thought: "OK, so now we don't have to put up with him. All he does is get high on his medicines anyway." I had not regarded my husband's prescription drug usage as "getting high," but I guess you could look at it that way. I was slowly opening my eyes.

I spoke to my clients that week about what was going on without too many details. I was embarrassed. This was not something I was proud of or wanted anyone to know. I just told them my husband and I were having problems, and we were separated now. I did not want pity from anyone. My mask was still on. Professionally, I felt I needed it.

Sunday night turned into Monday. I had not been able to sleep all night. I was worried about going to court and facing my husband. I had tried distracting myself with TV, but I could not focus on the stories on the screen. I had tried to meditate, but my thoughts got the better of me. My thoughts were running like a train out of control, and I was even more exhausted. I got up feeling light-headed, and I struggled to get ready. I wore a beige business suit. I had not worn that suit in years, and it looked baggy on me. I realized how much weight I had lost. I used a safety pin to fold my skirt on the side to prevent it from sliding down off me.

My substitute covered for me while I was in court. I had no lawyer, no one by my side. I had no friends to call. It was very lonely not having anyone to talk to. I had yet to tell my parents about my situation. Our relationship was very strained. I could use support, but I felt I would not get any support from them. (I had moved out of my parents' house when I was barely sixteen-years-old. Twenty years later, my mom still threw that in my face. We could not come to peace as to my reasons for leaving, but that is a story for another time.)

The courthouse was just off Main Street, and when I entered, I was again greeted by the guards and security personnel. One said, "Your husband just arrived." I dreaded facing him, and I had to find the strength to stand up to him.

As I mentioned earlier, over the years, I had become meek, small, and quiet. I lost my voice. My husband had manipulated me until I was a shadow of myself. Later, I learned this conditioning and grooming were methods abusers used to control their subjects.

I took the elevator downstairs to the courtroom and signed in. There were a lot of PFA cases. Plaintiffs were taken into the court-room, while the defendants remained in the hallway until they were called. It was 'standing room only' filled. Thankfully, I did not see him in the hallway. He must have been in the bathroom at that moment.

I walked into the courtroom and took a seat all by myself in the back row. I shivered with fear. I was nervous and felt like I needed to use the bathroom, but I was too scared to go into the hallway for fear of running into him. Someone tapped my shoulder and startled me. I must have looked like a deer facing headlights. A woman from Women's Resources was there to support me. I recognized her from my volunteer work with the agency, and I was grateful for a familiar face. She took me aside to let me know the order of events in court and to let me know she was there for me. It was a relief to have someone present alongside me. She gave me a hug. The human physical contact gave me strength. (Hugs release endorphins and help people heal.) It calmed me just enough, so I wasn't shaking anymore.

I sat back down and waited for my name to be called. There were two tables in the front. One was for the defendants and the other for plaintiffs. Most people had lawyers with them. I had not thought of hiring anyone. In the meantime, I heard many cases before mine. This was hard. Some people were escorted in handcuffs. Some people screamed at each other despite being in court. (So many secretive things happen behind closed doors in our neighbors' homes. We have no idea how anyone else truly lives.)

'When my name was called, I was asked to stand in front of the judge. My husband was escorted into the room, and he stood to my right. A public defender was by his side. My husband kept looking at me and sneering. I watched him peripherally and felt his gaze boring into me. The judge spoke to him and directed him to not look in my direction. She gave him one warning. He apologized profusely and theatrically. Then he turned to me to apologize "for looking at my wife." His sarcasm was not lost on the judge who warned him, once again, not to look at me or he would be held in contempt.

I raised my right hand and swore "to tell the truth and nothing but the truth." I stated my full name to confirm we were married. I was directed to speak up and speak clearly. I was speaking very softly. I was extremely scared. The judge then asked me to state the reason for seeking a permanent PFA. I started speaking and was advised to speak up again. My hands shook so much that I locked them together to make the shaking stop. A snide remark came from my husband's direction. The judge did not hear him, but his public defender admonished him quietly.

Into the microphone, I said, "Your Honor, on July fourth, my husband broke my ribs."

"That's not true. She's lying. How dare she," he retorted. "She just wants my house." The judge slammed down the gavel. She commanded my husband to be quiet or be removed from the courtroom.

I tried to continue. "I was in bed when it happened, after we had a horrible fight." This was all I was able to say. At that moment, there was commotion from my husband. He was clutching his chest and breathing hard.

I instinctively ran to his side as he fell to the floor. He had a history of heart issues and, throughout the years, I frequently tended him like a nurse. I felt torn. How could I leave him when he was in pain? I worried for my husband. Women's Resources' staff gently advised me to take a deep breath and step away from him so the officers could take a look at him. The paramedics brought a stretcher. Meanwhile, the judge called for a recess. She asked my husband if he needed a continuance to go to the hospital. He responded that because of his health, the case should be dropped. He demanded he be allowed to return to his house for his care. In addition, he threatened to sue the court if they listened to my lies.

The paramedics took his blood pressure. It was 140/90. High for some people, but his blood pressure usually ran much higher. This reading was his norm. His heartbeat was steady and normal, too. The judge made it clear that because of the disturbance he caused, there would be no continuance. In fact, the hearing would be held whether my husband was present or not. He hollered from the stretcher for the judge "to stop and desist now. You will be sued if you continue and I'm not here." He was wheeled away and taken to Pocono Medical Center.

The judge asked if I was ready to continue after a short recess. I regarded her, bewildered. "Without him present?"

"Yes."

I took a bathroom break to gain my composure. Of all the scenarios I had thought could be possible, I never imagined my husband would be riding in an ambulance on his way to the hospital during the hearing. The Women's Resources worker hugged me, and we walked into the courtroom together. I was reminded by the court that I had already been sworn in and I was asked to state the reasons for being there. I told the judge everything: my fears, my pain, his threats, my hospital visit, and the endless fights. I spilled it all—in public. The courtroom was filled with people. They heard me. They were listening. There were no other distractions in the courtroom. I was the only one speaking and stripping myself naked layer by layer down to my soul. I felt the shame of having lived like this. I cried while I talked. I presented the discharge papers from the hospital confirming I had three broken ribs. I begged the judge to add the boys to the PFA.

The judge granted three years of protection from abuse for me and my children. I had to ask her to further explain the order. I was in shock. She clarified my husband was not to come in contact with any one of us or enter the house again. His items could be picked up by a third party. I regarded the sincerity in the judge's eyes when she said, "I wish you the best. Be strong for yourself and your children. You have the strength in you." I thanked her. I thanked everyone from Women's Resources as well. Their emotional support meant the world to me.

I had not realized how lonely and isolated I had been. Being friendless is like being on an island with no phone. My entire personal life had revolved around my husband, and now he was gone. I had no girlfriends to confide in. I did not have a cousin or another family member to talk to. My life had been cut off from the outside world, except for my clients.

Despite everything that he had done, I was extremely worried about my husband. I needed to know he was OK. I called the hospital to inquire about his condition, but I didn't want to speak to him. I was told he had ridden in the ambulance to the emergency room but had refused treatment. He hassled the hospital staff so much that the attendant immediately recognized his name when I asked about him. He had walked out and was on his way to the hotel.

Talk about feeling deceived. He had tried to stop the hearing by exploiting his poor health, and he had effectively played into my emotions, proving he still had control over me. Although I had won the PFA, I had lost to him. He still controlled my emotions. I longed to be free of his manipulations. Maybe I had Stockholm syndrome? Maybe I related to him too much? His spectacle in court finally awakened me to his calculated manipulations. Here I was concerned about my husband and his health, and it had never occurred to me he could be faking. He had real health issues yet, that day, that precise day, he refused medical treatment and walked five miles from the hospital to the hotel in the summer heat. Obviously, he was not that ill. It was an eye-opening experience for me and helped me make a clean mental and emotional break from him.

I arranged for an acquaintance to take the court order and his personal belongings to the hotel, so he was made aware of the stipulations the judge had imposed on him.

I decided to have lunch by myself before heading back to work and home. This was a new experience for me. I enjoyed the freedom. I needed some breathing time to gain composure. At a local restaurant, I ordered a salad and called my sister-in-law. I filled her in on the details of the morning. She was grateful I was safe and advised me to think of the future now. I did not know where to start, but at least I was free and safe.

I then called my parents in New York. I had anticipated a very hard conversation. I had assumed that my mother would judge me. Incredibly, she listened attentively. She told me she had known all along what kind of man my husband was and was not surprised. She was glad the boys and I were okay. It felt very nice to have called her.

My parents promised to visit soon. By the time I returned home that afternoon, I felt drained. And stressed. The childcare parents noticed the change in me, and some questioned the new circumstances. I had no reason to hide anything anymore. Mask off. I gave them the details, and they were shocked to hear them. They said they had no idea any abuse had been taking place. No one knew. We hid our problems very well.

They appreciated he was out of the house, but they were worried he may return while their kids were in my care. All I could do was present the PFA. One of my clients was a cop, so he made a point of alerting the precinct about my situation. However, I had already made that call when my husband had been removed a week ago. Fortunately, we were among the precinct's top priorities when it came to protection. My husband was too smart, though, to do anything while children were present. He had his image to maintain. He was very careful about that. There was no way he was ever going to show the world his true self.

According to the tales my husband was telling, he was the victim who had been forcibly removed from his house for no reason. He was ill and needed his nurse. He was innocent, and I just wanted to steal his house. I did not hear from him all summer.

12

SUMMER OF 2010

THE SUMMER OF 2010 WAS the best summer I remember ever having in my life. We were happy at home. The dark cloud that had hung over our heads was lifted. I was free to think. I did not need to check in with anyone regarding my decisions. No one walked on eggshells. The boys had friends over in the afternoons. This was a first for everyone. It was fun, lazy summer—the way they should be.

I started a true love affair—with myself. I learned about me all over again. I took time to give myself manicures. I meditated and read. I wanted me. I learned to look in the mirror and see who I was. There were so many things I needed to change about myself, and these changes would take time. I desired to heal from the inside out.

My birthday in late July was memorable. I took the boys hiking. I walked along the trail, while they ran through the woods and jumped over boulders. They chased each other, laughed, and fell. I watched my boys, grateful to have them in my life. After hiking, we enjoyed front-row seats at a Triple-A Yankees game in Scranton. Watching baseball was one of our favorite activities as a family. This time, we had no stress. No one yelled at us or belittled us as had been the norm when my husband joined us. That evening, I took my boys to a hibachi dinner—fun and entertaining. I even bought myself flowers. I went to bed that night with a smile on my face.

Buying myself flowers was something new for me. There was no reason why I needed someone to buy me anything. These were lessons I was learning. My happiness was solely on me. I had to find my own way and get strong for my boys; they were counting on me. In the morning, I smelled the flowers in the room when I woke up, and I smiled again. Life was peaceful. A parent from childcare mentioned I looked happy and should smile more because it made me look less serious. I had not realized how the outside world perceived me. Later that month, I treated myself to a necklace I admired at Kay Jewelers. It felt great to buy myself a piece of jewelry.

My ribs still hurt when I coughed, sneezed, or moved too quickly. I was careful to avoid lifting or carrying any child while I healed. I took morning walks through the neighborhood to get fresh air and think. It was quiet, and homes were spread very far apart. Trees and creeks were everywhere. Early one morning, as I was strolling, a flock of turkeys scared me with their noisy procession in front of me. They chased me down the road. I must have looked like a crazy woman, shrieking with a flock of turkeys gobbling behind her. They were very noisy and rambunctious. Country life. I loved it.

I was busy with my children and the childcare. My substitute continued to help me while I was healing. It felt great to turn on music with the kids and watch them dance like no one was watching. Kids have a way of seizing life in the moment. They danced with abundant energy. Laughed hysterically. Jumped with all of their might. And they played intensely. That is why when their games are interrupted, their lives are interrupted.

That summer was idyllic, but it was time to plan my future. I inquired about divorce fees at a couple law firms, and attorneys were honest enough to share that Pennsylvania, a commonwealth, could draw out a divorce for as many as 10 years! Pennsylvania considers all assets and debts acquired during a marriage as community or marital property and, therefore, subject to division. But because the house was built and bought before me, it was only my husband's. I also needed to have his consent for a divorce. He could drag it out for a long time, thus the high costs for litigation. A few lawyers did not want to take my case because of conflicts of interest. They knew my husband or myself on a professional level. One attorney acquaintance mentioned I could get an uncontested divorce in New York if I was a resident there for two years. This was the first time I considered moving back to New York. I had lived in Pennsylvania for 16 years. I did not see this as a possibility unless my parents helped me.

I investigated changing the deed of the house to my name or adding my name to it. I could not do either without my husband's signed permission. I talked with the mortgage company about adding my name as a payer since I had a long history of making the payments. Again, no changes were allowed unless my husband signed off on them. He would never sign over the house, and he would contest the divorce. Tough decisions needed to be made. I questioned my reasons for staying in Pennsylvania.

Was I going to stay to fight for a house that held bad memories? Was I willing to fight for a house that was not in my name after all three boys were grown-ups? Gabe was 17, and Peter was 16. In less than two years, they would both, technically, be adults. Who knew if they would still want to live with me? They both wanted to go away for college. Was I willing to start over? This was a big decision. I did not want to live in my husband's shadow.

Slowly, I came to the conclusion I should move. It would be difficult, but the choice made sense. I would need to close the business I ran for 11 years, so moving meant losing home *and* business. Life, as I had known it, would be over.

My father came to visit me for a week in August. It was nice having him. We got a chance to talk and spend time together. I felt like I connected with my father like I never had before, and the bond made a huge difference to me. My father walked around the house and property with me, and we talked about nothing and everything. My relationship with him had always been great, but, unfortunately, due to his hearing loss, our conversations were best done in person. If I called him, he could not hear me well.

"Papi, como estas?" (Dad, how are you?)

He would answer: "How are the kids? Are you OK?" "I'm OK. How are you?"

"The weather is OK here too," he would respond.

Lack of proper communication meant fewer phone calls. Sometimes, the conversations could be funny if they weren't so sad. As we walked around the house and property, he noted all the improvements he had made: a finished basement with a game room for the boys, fencing around the backyard, and a third floor that was converted from one large room into two bedrooms. He had completed much of the work on the property, and now we were walking away from it. However, my father agreed with me that it was time to move on, time to move to New York with them. The necessity did not negate how hard the move was going to be. This home was the only one the boys could remember.

My parents allowed us to move in with them. That was a big relief. I would occupy my old bedroom in the basement, and the boys would settle into their own rooms on the third floor. We talked endlessly about how we would make this work. The older boys would finish school at John Browne High School, where my brother worked as a biology teacher and served as department head. My youngest, John, would go to my old elementary school, Our Lady Queen of Martyrs.

Decision made. It seemed like the transition would be smooth. I had a mandatory meeting with each parent in August regarding the closing of the childcare on September 30, 2010. I also distributed written notices. It was a heartbreaking decision, but the right one. I had built my childcare from nothing and made it into the highest quality childcare in my area. It was something I was extremely proud of. I knew I would continue working with kids on some level in the future. The local paper wrote one last story on the closing of my childcare. I tried so hard during the interview to not to break down in tears.

One client family generously offered to pay the upfront costs for a new childcare center in town, so I would not move out of Pennsylvania. They did not want anyone but me caring for their children. I thought long and hard about the generous offer, but I knew in my heart it was time to leave the Poconos. I wanted to be far away from my husband. If I started another business in town, I would require an apartment nearby and I would be too close to him. The laws in Pennsylvania prevented me from obtaining a divorce without his consent. The new business would be considered his since we were married.

The decision to move would affect my boys. It was Gabriel's senior year in high school and his last soccer season. I told him he could live with my substitute, Liz, and finish the school year. Yet, Gabriel felt that he needed to be with me to ensure I would be OK. I never realized he had stepped into the role as the man of the house after my husband was forced out. I hoped he would not regret his decision to move with us. I attempted to change his mind a couple times. He conceded to stay in Pennsylvania until the end of soccer season. Then, he would join us in New York. Peter considered the move a new adventure and looked forward to it.

John was a problem. First, he said all rivers in New York were filled with "dead bodies from mob kills." He also stated he could not breathe in New York because "they have no fresh air." He was born and raised in Pennsylvania. He had three adult brothers and a sister from his father's side there, too. But at 11 years old, he needed to follow my lead as his mother.

I was making a leap of faith with the boys who relied on me. We were moving from the only house they knew into my parents' small house. I would need a job outside of the home. I read job postings online, and I was qualified for several. I really was not worried about employment. I had a degree and a lot of work experience, and with these two attributes, I could get myself on my feet again. I had learned a life lesson years ago when I had lived in a shelter.

* * *

Angela's Advice

You can lose your material possessions, but no one can take away what's inside your mind or heart.

* * *

THE MONTH of September was bittersweet—my last month working as a family childcare provider. I cherished every hug and smile from the children. I memorized their faces, and I took a lot of photos. Closing my business was harder than I thought. I was closing a chapter in my life that meant everything to me. My childcare turned me into a professional. I was frequently dehydrated that month from all my crying. I only shed tears once for my marriage, but my professional life was different. Closing my business was crushing my spirit and causing me so much sorrow. I was losing the biggest part of me by closing my child care. More than once, I nearly changed my mind. I had no idea it was going to get much worse for me.

I requested a meeting with my husband through a therapist. (We were not allowed to have any contact, so this meeting required permission. There was no way I could risk anything by telling him without someone present anyway.) I would tell him I was leaving the house and closing the business. On the third Friday in September, I arrived at the therapist's office first. My husband walked in with a smile on his face. "I'm glad you wanted to meet. I guess this means we can get back together again. When am I moving back in?" he asked. I dropped the bomb, and he flipped over the coffee table. He attempted to grab me, but the table legs blocked him. He almost tripped. He screamed, "You can't leave me. What about the business? You love your work. You would never close the business." His mask had come off.

I told him the closing date had been set. He had counted on me never closing the business, but September 30th, 2010 was my last day. It was over. The therapist directed him to leave, or she would call the cops and building security. He left—shrieking and cursing me out. She asked me to wait to leave until we were assured he had left the parking lot. She advised me he was volatile and had nothing to lose. I needed to be careful.

I witnessed a very scary side of my husband. He had lost all control. I drove home, worried about what he might do. I did not have long to wait and wonder. He called me several times that night —cursing me out and swearing. Around 11 p.m. when I was in bed, I heard banging at the front door. My dog Sonny barked at the startling noise. My husband screamed and wailed that I could not ever leave him and I could not survive without him. "You belong to me." He had completely lost it. I did not open the door. I called the cops. Officers took him to jail for violating the PFA.

The following Monday morning, I was back in court. This time, I knew a little better what to expect. I *thought* I was ready to see him, but he was brought in handcuffs. Ironically, he appeared more threatening in cuffs. We were both sworn in, and the charges for violating the protection order were stated. My husband was adamant: The PFA was invalid because he had never agreed to it, nor was he present for the hearing. The judge made it clear that his permission was not needed for a PFA. After listening to the case, the judge allowed the time served in jail to be his sentence. She also extended the PFA until John was 18. I was asked if I had any other notices to give to my husband. I told him there was a custody hearing coming up the first week of October. My husband glowered at me and sneered, "You will not win that one."

The judge reminded him that no contact was allowed with me or the boys. Adjustments could only be made during the custody hearing. I would find out, during the custody hearing, if the PFA would stand up. The judge made it clear my husband would be locked up immediately—and for a longer period—if he approached me in any manner again. My husband realized now the judge was serious, and he left me alone. He saw the change in me that day. He could no longer manipulate me. Maybe it was the way I walked or held myself. As I departed the courtroom, he said, "You are not the same person." I'm glad I wasn't. He recognized that my strength was returning.

13

GIO

DURING MY CHILDHOOD, GIO, SHORT for Giovanni, was a thorn in my side at every family gathering. He broke my toys, pulled my pigtails, and just acted rambunctious. Our mothers were great friends before either one of us were born, and our families were close. However, after he moved to Italy with his parents when he was 9, I forgot all about him. He returned to the States as a teenager and lived with my aunt and uncle (his godparents) in East Hampton, NY while finishing high school. I learned he was living there, but I did not want to visit him—I remembered how he was.

When he got married, though, I had to be present because the rest of the family, except his mother, had boycotted the wedding. I knew what it was like to have few family members share such an important day. Only my aunt, uncle, and one cousin attended my first wedding. Everyone else had boycotted my first wedding, too.

His mother cried for him at the wedding. While she was freshening up in the bathroom, she explained that she had to attend her son's wedding, whether she was happy for him or not. I told her that her presence at his wedding would be remembered and appreciated.

Through the years, Gio and I were sometimes in contact at Christmas. When my husband and I were still together, we had been trying to get closer by gathering annually for New Year's at our house in Pennsylvania. In 2010 New Year's, he told me he was very happy because he and his second wife were trying to have a baby, and they were looking to buy a house. I was ecstatic for him. He had been with his second wife for several years already, and these seemed like the logical next steps.

His wife was pouring herself a drink and watching everyone play games in the game room. I congratulated her on the news. She responded, "That's what *he* wants." I did not know how to respond to that statement, so I just kept eating chips. I was dumbfounded and just kept stuffing my mouth with food. The conversation was now awkward because we were not close enough to continue it. I also could not tell Giovanni what his wife had said. I was not comfortable enough to share that conversation.

The couple visited us again the following month. Gio skied with my boys, and his wife snowboarded. Poconos, a well-known ski resort area, made a great stop during Gio's ski vacation. At this time, my husband and I were having issues. I declined Gio's ski invitation by declaring my husband was ill. Meanwhile, he was just in a horrible mood and did not want me to go skiing. My husband iterated that I was too old for things like that, and I had too many responsibilities to allow myself to get hurt skiing.

That was the last time I spoke with Gio until September 2010. On September 10, Gio and his mother came for a visit. His mother, Genoveva, lived in Italy, and it was nice seeing her after more than 18 years. I learned from my mother he had broken up with his second wife. Gio told me that during his previous ski visit, they had already split up, but he had wanted to keep up appearances. He had worn his mask in front of me. Ironically, I was wearing a mask then, too.

Gio and I discussed our exes. Neither of us was ready to date or even get to know new people. We laughed at the thought of speed dating or blind dates. We talked about how horrible first dates could be. After two marriages each, neither one of us wanted a new relationship. And I had three boys—a lot of baggage for anyone to take on. In addition, my personal and professional lives were completely starting over, and I needed to think about me.

Gio had never had a child with either wife, so part of him felt he was missing out on fatherhood. He had resigned himself to the fact he would never be a father. He lived in Little Italy in the Bronx—in the same building where his parents had lived in the early 1980s. His life was simple now. He went to work and came home. Gio had reconciled himself to working long hours and returning to an empty apartment. He had lost a lot of weight since February. He told me I looked skinny, too.

He had been dealing with a big loss of his own. Gio's second wife had suddenly told him she wanted to "find" herself and move on. He could not understand why she wanted to leave because to him, "I do" meant forever. Regardless, it was an amicable divorce. They even had lunch together and talked about their taxes that year.

Gio's mother said her good-nights, then walked away, mumbling "no ven nada." ("They don't see anything.") I had no idea what she was talking about. Not until later did it dawn on me that she saw something neither one of us had seen—something right in front of our eyes. Meanwhile, the boys were getting rowdy downstairs, so I headed to the game room to see what was going on. Their game playing was turning to bickering. It was almost midnight, which was extremely late, so I sent them to bed.

But I was not tired, and neither was Gio. He suggested watching a movie downstairs in the game room. We went through my DVD selections. He had never watched *Pursuit of Happiness* with Will Smith, one of my favorite inspirational movies. We stayed up to watch the movie. It felt nice to sit and watch a good movie on the futon with a friend. I got a blanket to cover ourselves because it was chilly. Gio offered his shoulder to lean on, and it felt natural to put my head there. He rubbed my head with his hands and ran his fingers through my hair. When he put his hand over my hand, I felt something I had never felt before. Indigestion? Heartburn? Nerves? I felt something in my stomach.

We turned toward each other, and his expression mirrored my feeling of shock. It was a what-the-hell-is-going-on look. I backed away. My face was too close to his. We were in each other's personal space. I excused myself to use the bathroom. I needed to regroup, figure out what was going on. I looked at myself in the mirror, I reprimanded myself out loud: "Stop this. You are a grown woman, not a teenager. You are a mother. You consider him to be a cousin. This is not a game. You are not going to have a fling or an affair with this man." It was kind of silly, but I needed that talking to by my own conscience out loud.

As a mother, I modeled the right behavior, and the idea of a fling with Gio was just completely foreign to me. This was a man whom I'd known my whole life. Our lives and families had always been intermingled. We were both barely out of our long relationships.

On top of everything, though, I had not had any real affection or love in years. I had accepted this part of my life. I had been celibate for years because of my husband's bad moods and poor health. I never thought about it or felt a need for it. I could not think of opening myself to anyone. Yet, here I was, talking to myself in the bathroom mirror. I could not let lust control my behavior. I walked back downstairs with solid determination to be firm and not turn this moment into anything bigger. Besides, it could all be my imagination. Why would Gio want to get together with someone with so many issues, especially now that I had confided in him about my dire circumstances? My husband would be a thorn in my side for years to come—PFA or not.

Gio asked if I was OK after I returned, and he wondered what took me so long. I guess my private talk with myself took longer than I thought. I sat down quietly next to him on the futon. He held one of my hands and tipped my chin up to his face. I had no idea what was going on in his head. My brain went blank. He gazed deeply into my eyes—then slowly, he kissed me on the lips. Soft at first, questioning almost, then long and hard with passion as if he answered his own question. I had never been kissed this way before. So much for being strong, I thought. I gave in to his mouth and his hands. I responded.

It felt incredible, and I could not think. All thoughts of restraint left my head. His mouth and hands felt somehow familiar and new at the same time. I was enveloped in his strength. There was no awkwardness. While he was kissing and caressing my neck and shoulders, I stopped him. Barely.

We were both starving for each other, starving for affection and it showed. It felt like coming home, being in his arms and feeling his body next to mine.

When I was 11 and Giovanni was 8, we kissed for the first time. It was a child's hesitant sweet innocent peck of a kiss. It was my first kiss. We kissed in his aunt's bedroom during a New Year's Eve party. His mother walked in on us and we jumped away from each other and never talked about it. I barely remembered it. He had learned quite a few things since that first kiss. He had become an expert kisser, using his mouth in ways I never knew possible. It was very exciting.

We needed to talk now. We couldn't just act without thinking this through. We both agreed this was different. We were crossing into unchartered waters. This was more than just us or even my boys. It could not be just a fling. Our families would be involved. Whether we wanted to believe it or not, many factors needed to be considered if we started anything. Neither one of us wanted to have a one-night stand or a simple affair but moving into a relationship was something we were not ready for either.

We were honest and unmasked ourselves to each other while we talked through the night. It was the kind of conversation that holds nothing back. We got naked, not physically, but to our souls that night. I found strength in that. Once we were stripped of everything superficial, we were vulnerable and capable of seeing each other as we really were. We became one in mind and thought that night.

It wasn't until I heard the boys get up that I realized we had been talking through the entire night. I wasn't the least bit tired. We walked upstairs and made breakfast for everyone. I had not pulled an all-nighter since my college days when I crammed for exams. I felt different and energized. My boys found me smiling in the kitchen. They teased me, and they wondered why I was smiling. The night before, Gio told me he always thought I was a serious person. He never understood the sadness that was in my heart. And that morning was the first time he saw me smile and laugh. "I never realized," he said. No one had realized.

Gio pulled his old pranks, reminding me of how long I had known him. He used the hose from the kitchen faucet to start a water fight with the boys and me. There was water everywhere and laughter, too. We slipped and fell. We chased each other around the house with water cups. I ran into my bedroom and closed the door to escape being soaked by my boys. I heard Gio knock on the door, begging to come in, but I refused to open it. I knew I would only get splashed in the face! We were all soaked when it was over. All the stress and tension we were feeling dissipated that morning with his antics—at least for a little while.

Gio's face is one I grew up with. Our lives had always been intertwined. When he split up with his first wife, he had lived with my parents in my old room, sleeping in my childhood bed. I had not been speaking to my parents at that time because this was when I was living in a shelter, and I had not known his circumstances.

Life had a funny way of going in circles. All I knew was I was falling hard for a man I had known all my life. This feeling was something completely unexpected, but, then again, one never knows when love might come into a person's life. Love. That seemed impossible. And it was the wrong time to think about love. I was vulnerable. We both knew beginning a relationship with sex could be regrettable. We should be sure of where the relationship was going before getting physical. We were not ready to make that step.

No one from the outside would possibly understand our new relationship. It looked like a rebound for both of us. We agreed to take it slow and talk some more. I was moving to my parents' house in Queens in a month, and we could see each other in New York. We still had a lot to learn about each other. My boys and securing a job were my priorities. I had a lot to sort through in my life. One decision we made that night was to stop calling each other "cousins," which was a hard, but necessary, habit to break. I made a mental change to refer to him as Giovanni instead of Gio. (The boys continued to call him Gio.)

Giovanni and his mother left that morning to visit a friend in the neighborhood. We had agreed to be discreet about our feelings at this point. No one knew what was going on. We did not really know what was going on either. My boys suspected something was different, though, and they teased me.

Giovanni and I had nightly phone conversations, getting to know each other more. I looked forward to our long phone calls.

14

THE END OF MY CHILDCARE
BUSINESS

THE LAST WEEK OF SEPTEMBER arrived too quickly. I had given freely to crying now at the end of the day. I was not eating too well either. I was going to miss my childcare kids and families. Everyone was very supportive. On the last Friday afternoon of September, I was invited on a ride with a client, Michael. When I was in his car, I was blindfolded. I had never been blindfolded before, so this was different and somewhat scary. Michael asked me to trust him. My concepts of time and place were muddled because of the blindfold. Peter was in the back seat; he assured me that I was going to like where we were going.

We arrived at our destination after driving around for a bit. I was walked through a room and hallway. I heard whispers and giggles all around me. When I took off the blindfold, I was surrounded by the families and children I had cared for throughout the years. Faces I had not seen in a long time were there. Everywhere I turned, there was another former family and child.

Children—all grown up—surrounded me and gave me hugs. The ruse, driving me around, allowed everyone to set up for the party. My blindfolded entry into my own house through the garage made it unfamiliar.

Peter had gone through my business files and contacted everyone. He was very thoughtful. He understood well what I was feeling. The party featured a great potluck spread. We reminisced. The families asked me about my plans for New York. Then, they wished me well.

At the end of this incredible, memorable night, we said our heartfelt goodbyes. I knew I would never see these families again. They had taken time out of their lives to show me how much my work had meant to them. I hoped we could remain in touch somehow, but we all knew how time and place could separate lives. This chapter of my life was over.

A couple families lingered. They asked if I wanted to go out. I did not know what they meant. Literally, go out? They wanted to take me out for drinks. I had not gone out for drinks since I was single. That meant over 20 years ago. I did not think that going out for drinks was something that someone my age did—especially a mom of three boys. My sons overheard the conversation, and they convinced me to join the group. They wanted me to have fun.

I always kept a respectful, professional distance from my clients. Clients could not be friends because I was working for them. I was careful about only being professionally friendly. But the business was closed, so my personal policy no longer applied. I could hang out with them and have fun. Michelle and her sister, Chriselle, helped me dress. These two sisters had their children in my care for over six years. They went through my wardrobe to find something appropriate. I really did not own anything they deemed sexy. My clothes were (and still are) conservative. They helped me with my makeup and hair. When I looked in the mirror, I saw a different person looking back. I looked like my face belonged in a magazine. I had always sought a natural look when applying makeup, so this was completely different, but so was going out. I needed the change.

Michael, his wife, Kelli, Joy, Nicole, Alexandra, Michelle, and

Chriselle (all former clients) took me to a local bar called Front Row on Main Street, where we danced and drank. I had not had a drink in a long time, unless you count church wine on Sundays. One drink got me tipsy, but I had fun dancing and singing. They were teaching me I was still young despite being 40 and could have fun. It was memorable. I let my guard down and allowed myself to have a good time. When the night was over, I went home with special gifts and memories that have lasted me a lifetime. Kelli later told me: "I never knew that someone could be in such a shell until that night. You were like a caterpillar in a cocoon, and you turned into a butterfly overnight." Michelle made a point to call and check up on me the next day. She also set up a time to do highlights in my hair.

Giovanni visited the following weekend. He wanted to spend time with us before we were uprooted. While Michelle did my hair, he played video games with the boys. I strolled into the living room with a new outfit and a new hairstyle (both thanks to Michelle). The boys and Giovanni did not recognize me at first. Michelle suggested that Giovanni take me out. The boys kidded me a bit, then they realized that something was happening between Giovanni and me. We went to the Front Row because I did not know any other bar in town. Giovanni said it was a quiet bar. I guess he was used to the bars in New York City on a Saturday night.

This was our first date. Most first dates are awkward and almost like interviews. (What do you do? What are your parents like? Do you have siblings?)

We knew all this information about each other. My brother, Hernando, and Giovanni had been friends for years and had hung out many times. I had recently been re-introduced to his sister, Pamela. She was much younger than Giovanni. Pamela was born in Italy, and she lived most of her life there with their parents. We chatted about our recent activities and got to know each other even better. Giovanni spent the night in the guest room and left for New York in the morning.

The first week of October, I had a hearing to request permission to relocate to New York with my youngest son John. I felt cold during the hearing. Something was going on with my health, but I did not know or have time to deal with it now. I thought it was just nerves because I was facing my husband again. I felt light-headed, and that reminded me I had forgotten, once again, to eat breakfast or lunch. Did I have dinner the night before? Some women eat when they are upset. I do the opposite.

The judge listened to both sides. My husband was adamantly opposed to allowing me to take his son with me. I presented to the court my reasons for moving and explained the familial support system I would have there. My husband made a point to say: "You will not last a month with your mother. You two have too many issues." I offered information regarding John's school to the court, as well. The fact that he was switching from one private school to another private school was in my favor.

After a short deliberation, the judge granted me permission to relocate with my son. This moment was bittersweet. The last tie to Pennsylvania was severed. The custody agreement had been finalized. I advised my husband that I would be moving Columbus Day weekend. He could move back into the house after that.

Per the custody agreement, John would visit his father every other weekend. We would meet halfway at a mall in New Jersey for the exchange. The times and dates, including holidays, were set, as well. This schedule would be the new norm for John, and he was not happy. He stormed out of the courthouse ahead of me. John did not want to be with his father at all and he did not want to abandon his life in Pennsylvania either.

A couple days after the hearing, a doctor called to inform me that my husband tried to commit suicide and was on suicide watch. He was asking to see me. This was not a surprise to any of us. He had threatened suicide or had attempted suicide many times. I reminded the doctor of this. I also informed the doctor that I was no longer involved in his life. My husband's emergency contacts should be changed to his adult children or his sisters. The hospital staff had already contacted his family, but they did not want to be involved. The hospital had called me per my husband's request. I reported to them there was a PFA in place, and he could not have contact with me.

My husband was alone now—no one by his side. I felt sorry for him. Despite everything that had happened, I did not wish him ill. This man had an amazing extended family. My husband had five grown kids from a previous marriage as well as sisters, nieces, and nephews who were caring and wonderful people. However, he had effectively made himself into a pariah with his actions over the years.

I called my sister-in-law, and she confirmed she wanted nothing more to do with her brother and she was not going to be involved with him anymore. She extended her love to me and my boys and asked me to keep in touch. We did. John maintained contact with his father's side of the family. He had a lot of cousins, two aunts, plus his adult siblings from his father's side. The following year, we joined my sister-in-law at her beautiful beach house in New Jersey. In the 12 years I had been with my husband, we had never been invited. Now that I was not with him, I was invited. I found that ironic.

15

THE MOVE

MOVING INTO MY PARENTS' HOUSE in Queens meant we had to give up a lot of items. Space was limited. Most importantly, we needed to give up a number of our pets. My mother was not happy about any animals in her house and we had a lot of pets. I called the local nature center to take my two 5-foot iguanas. We had built a beautiful habitat for them. We loved them very much, but we could not possibly care for them at my parents' house. When the nature center staff picked up the iguanas, they also took my turtles. I had owned those turtles for more than 15 years. I was going to miss them dearly.

My four doves went to an aviary specialist. The fish tank went to a friend. Our cat Peaches went to John's sister, because Peaches had been her cat in the first place. (She had adopted the cat as a kitten while she was living with us.) Unfortunately, of all the animals, Peaches was the one that did not fare well. Her only home had been our house, and she escaped from John's sister's home and never returned. Only our old golden retriever Sonny, Peter's cockatiel, four hand-raised pet rats, and John's bearded dragon moved to New York.

The plan was to put the childcare items into storage. Other child-cares in the area offered to buy items, so I sold some furniture and supplies. I needed the money. My dad and Giovanni helped with the packing. It was overwhelming to see my business being packed up and sealed away. I sat down in the middle of the playroom floor and just bawled like a child. It hit me hard that this part of my life was over. My sobs shook my body. My father, not used to emotional outbursts, hugged me and walked me out of the room. He told me to go lay down while he worked on the packing and stowing away all of the supplies. It hurt too much to do these tasks myself. I just wanted to curl up in a ball in bed.

Everything was boxed—every book, every toy, every doll, every block, every Lego, every instrument, every poster, and every bin. All of my life work—packed and sealed in boxes.

I stored the childcare items because it was too hard to get rid of everything. There was no reason to leave the childcare furniture to my husband. Michael, my old client, lent us his truck to move the items into the storage unit in town. When everything was in storage, the finality of the moment hit me harder. My professional life was over. The storage unit door slammed shut and was locked. I took the key and walked away. Eleven years of work was now in a storage unit, and my heart broke.

I left the household items for my husband. We did not have much more to pack other than our clothes, books, my childhood piano, photos, mementos, and some personal items to take with us to New York. The boys did not need their bedroom furniture or desks. I was not taking anything from my bedroom, living room, or dining room. My parents' house had everything and was small, so there was no need for the bedroom, deck, or living room furnishings.

During the packing, John rebelled and repeatedly disappeared into the woods. Gabriel and Peter did not listen to me. They acted out and fought amongst themselves. I had to intervene numerous times and felt at a loss. (Later in New York, my mother told me I needed to punish the boys for their bad behavior, and I should be stricter with them. I did not see how punishing them would help matters at all. I felt they were acting out their frustrations. All of us were upset. Our lives were falling apart.)

I had always believed in signs but had never really witnessed them. One weekend before the move, I was heading to New York. While driving through the Gap with the Delaware River on my right, I turned to see an eagle, gliding parallel to the car. It glided with me for several seconds, long enough for me to see its beauty and strength. The eagle was flying east toward New York. At this same time, Bob Marley's song, "No Woman, No Cry," played on the radio. I was forced to pull over at the rest area. I felt like these signs were telling me I was driving toward my freedom. I needed to take in the moment. The symbol of the eagle never escaped me. In future months, I would remember this eagle well.

It was a hard couple of weeks. Columbus Day weekend had arrived too quickly. Among the personal items I retained were my children's papers, drawings, and stuffed animals. I could not deny my boys or myself these things, considering all we were giving up. Keeping some of the old stuff was the least I could do.

Giovanni and my father came up that weekend to help me pack. My dad said I looked pale. This move was emotionally draining. Giovanni prepared meals for us from scratch. He knew how to cook and not just one meal. As a bachelor, he had learned how to cook well. Also, his father had taught him how to make sauce from scratch. My father observed Giovanni in the kitchen and remarked, "His two wives let him get away? Why?" My dad was impressed by Giovanni's cooking skills. (My stomach was impressed too.) Being old-fashioned, my father was not used to seeing a man in the kitchen.

Giovanni had not cooked for a big family before. He said he enjoyed it. That weekend he prepared several meals and discovered how much teenage boys ate. My father was very sympathetic with me. He realized how hard this whole move was.

During the move, I also discovered that Giovanni was very meticulous and a good planner. We had just dumped stuff into the truck, but Giovanni had organized items to make things fit. He liked jigsaw puzzles, and that's what packing looked like to him.

The boys were becoming used to seeing Giovanni around. My father put his arm around him and thanked him for being there for us. Giovanni was proving to be a friend to us during this horrible time.

Before we departed on the Sunday of Columbus Day weekend, the boys and I said goodbye to Pennsylvania. I let them walk around the grounds one last time. They had their private goodbyes to the only home they had ever known.

During the move to New York, I drove the family Suburban with the kids and pets, while Giovanni and my dad rode in the U-Haul. Giovanni knew the boys were very upset about leaving their friends and home. He tried to make light of the situation by wagering on a race between the two vehicles. The road was rather empty because it was after rush hour. We should have been stopped by the cops on I-80 for speeding. The boys thought it was hysterical that we raced to get out of Pennsylvania. We arrived at my parents' house where my mother was waiting with lunch. Everyone unloaded the moving van.

Unfortunately, Giovanni and I needed to drive back to Pennsylvania to return the rented U-Haul, then drive back to New York with my second vehicle, a pickup truck. We arrived in Pennsylvania very late. Giovanni gave me space at the house. This time, I walked the halls alone. I went through each room, rekindling memories and reliving all the moments that had taken place in each one. I needed time to say goodbye to a house that was never truly mine. The walls looked bare.

Rooms echoed with memories. No children played with play-dough and laughed. No child read in the reading nook. The carpet had the indents from the bookshelves and piano. The walls had handprints— remnants of my work with children. The bedrooms still had furniture. The bathrooms had their knickknacks. The heart of the house had moved out, and only memories lingered, like ghosts.

Giovanni had fallen asleep on the couch while I did my final tour. My exhaustion from the weekend had caught up with me, and I sat down next to him and dozed off. Thankfully, an owl startled me after a short snooze. I realized we needed to be out of the house before morning. I did not want to see my husband, and he was coming back this day—that was the agreement. Giovanni and I left quickly. I walked away from the house, never looking back. I needed to look forward now.

We drove in silence. Giovanni was giving me space again. I desired time to process everything that was going on emotionally within me. We were both depleted from the physical labor and lack of sleep. Ten minutes into New Jersey, we were compelled to pull over to sleep in the truck in a strip mall parking lot for several hours. When we finally woke up, we picked up some breakfast at a fast-food restaurant, then got back on the road.

They say when you die, you see your life flash before you. In my case, I was seeing the past flash before me while we drove further away from Pennsylvania. So many hurtful memories with my husband came to mind. My perspective was now open. I had put myself in a bad situation and barely got out of it. I cried for the loss of my business. It had been the greatest achievement of my life. I felt lost now. My future was uncertain in every sense. What was I going to do? I had three grown boys who depended on me, and I had no clue what I was doing. I was trusting my parents to help me out, and I knew how hard that was going to be on them. Their lives were going to be deeply disrupted— seven people in a small house.

John later asked me: "Mom, why did you stay so long? Why?" I could only respond by explaining that I had been imprisoned in my mind. I had let myself be convinced I could not function without my husband. I had been locked into the house because the business was tied to it, as well. And my finances had been tied to the business. I also relayed to John that emotionally, I had not been strong. I wish I had been stronger earlier. I regretted not being a better, stronger mother to my boys.

16

NEW YORK

THIS WOULD HAVE BEEN ANOTHER nice point to end my story. We moved in, we adjusted, life went on. Happily-ever-afters had not existed in my life.

I took the big step of moving into my parents' house with the understanding we would live on the empty third floor until the tenants on the second floor vacated. Then, we would have our own apartment on the second floor. However, my brother and mother refused to let me and the boys live on the third floor because that would incur a code violation. There was no fire escape on the third floor. In addition, my parents' residence was registered as a two-family house. My parents had not asked the tenants on the second floor to leave, and they had no intention of doing so. This meant the boys got to flip a coin for the one couch in the living room, and the other two slept on the floor. My old bedroom in the basement could only fit a twin-size bed. The original arrangement never happened.

During our first week in New York, I enrolled the three boys in their respective schools, found doctors for us, opened a bank account, went to court to file the PFA, and spoke with an attorney about enforcing the PFA. I carried copies of the custody order and the PFA in my purse. In addition, I met with a previous client of mine, Luz, who worked at a local hospital.

Luz and I had kept in touch, and now I needed her help. She assisted me with filling out the healthcare forms to ensure my boys and I had state insurance. I cried in her arms in her office because my burdens were overwhelming. She told me things would change. "Things happen for a reason." I heard that a lot these days. I wished the reason would show itself soon because I was slowly breaking down. Thank goodness Luz was very comforting to me that day.

The older boys were enrolled in public school for the first time in their lives. I had to shop for new school clothes because they no longer would wear uniforms. Gabriel joined us in New York during the third week of October after soccer season ended. I had tried to convince him to finish his senior year in Pennsylvania, but he wanted to make sure I was OK. His decision upset me. I knew how hard it was for him to change schools during his senior year.

John pretended to gag when he left the house in the morning before school. He said he could not breathe the New York air because it was polluted. John was acting out horribly. He could not communicate with my mother because he had never been allowed to learn Spanish. (My husband had been adamant that we cease speaking Spanish because "we lived in the United States, not a Latino country.") I tried speaking Spanish, but when I did, my husband assumed I was talking about him behind his back, and I was being disrespectful. Our fights were endless about this topic. One time, my husband gave me the silent treatment for more than two weeks to make his point. He threatened to not take his medications if I continued speaking Spanish. John could have been bilingual like his brothers, which makes me regret losing that battle even more. They learned Spanish from me during their first four years, and they continued learning with their own father, my first husband.

John would leave the house without letting anyone know where he was going. This was not Pennsylvania where he could wander in the woods. There were nothing but row houses in Queens. He did not know the neighborhood or have a cell phone. He refused to discuss his feelings with me, but I could sense he was angry about his new life. He had a huge fight with my mother about our pets. My mother hated that we had brought animals to her house. She refused to let me have the rats anywhere near the first floor. They were banished to the third floor. Peter's bird was too noisy and rude, according to my mother. The bearded dragon was disgusting, she said.

Her biggest issue was with our beautiful, old golden retriever. Sonny was John's dog. He was 2 years old when he had picked out Sonny. They had grown up together, doing everything together. He had been a house dog, always with us. My mother adamantly refused to let us bring Sonny in the house past the mudroom. She banished him to the driveway or the mudroom. John repeatedly brought him inside to cuddle. Once, Sonny entered the kitchen, and my mother hollered at him just for being there. She hit him on his snout with a wooden spoon, which completely set off John. Sonny had never been hit or scolded in his life. John lost it with my mother and shrieked right back at her. My mother directed me to teach John respect. I let her know she needed to respect him and never hit animals.

This life required several enormous adjustments for all of us. We had no privacy and only one bathroom to share among seven people. (Our previous home had four bathrooms.) My older brother felt I had spoiled the boys, and they needed discipline. I thought otherwise. They needed love and understanding, not harsh punishments during this difficult transition. My brother called for lights out by 10 p.m. Hernando turned off their phones because he was (generously) paying our phone bills. After 10 p.m., my boys could not make any noise because my parents were sleeping in the next room. The early bedtime was something very new for them.

I went to bed by 10 p.m. the first week, as well. The house had only one old tube television, and it was in the living room. With the lights out, there was nothing to do but read or sleep. Sometimes, I spoke on the phone with Giovanni after lights out. At least my phone was not turned off. My brother eventually inquired about the additional minutes. He was monitoring my phone usage. I was grateful for the help with the phone bills and for a place to stay, but I felt like I had reversed time and was being treated like a child.

Arguments erupted nightly, daily, constantly among the boys. First, they were just verbal arguments. Then, the boys got physical with each other. The sleeping arrangements were far from ideal. The boys had been privileged to each have their own rooms in our old house. Sleeping on the floor or on the couch was a sad turn of events. My mother repeatedly made me feel like the worst mother in the world, claiming the boys' fighting was all my fault.

At the first chance, the three boys visited their respective fathers — Gabriel and Peter went to their father in Connecticut, and John went to Pennsylvania. None of them wanted to remain at my parents' for the weekend. The close quarters were really getting on everyone's nerves.

Giovanni invited me to go away with him that first weekend I was in New York since the boys were all with their fathers. He had two tickets to a wine festival in Virginia. He had been planning on taking a friend, but his friend had backed out. I had not gone away for a weekend with a guy that was not my husband, so this was new territory for me. I agreed to go but was very nervous. I knew what this weekend meant. We were taking our relationship to another level. We had already talked about being intimate, and each of us had gone for blood tests. That was something I did not mess around with. I knew of too many people who had gotten sick and even died from STD's.

That weekend with Giovanni, I could finish a sentence and even a thought without being interrupted by a child—very grown-up. During the long drive down to Virginia, we spent every minute talking. We discussed life—past, present, and future. Giovanni and I had no secrets from each other. We stopped to eat and spent even more time chatting. At the hotel, the receptionist asked if we wanted television service in the room. Giovanni responded, "That's not necessary. We will be too busy for TV." I was completely embarrassed, red in the face!

We settled into the room. Again, I was impressed with Giovanni's packing and organizational skills. He was so meticulous. I folded my clothes, but he pressed his clothes. We got comfortable and started to kiss passionately; then we stopped ourselves from anything further because I wanted to get something to eat first. Giovanni agreed. Secretly, I was postponing the bedroom activities for a bit.

We enjoyed dinner at an outdoor bistro. It felt nice to be with someone who wanted to be with me. Conversation flowed easily with us. I was palm-sweaty nervous about what was going to happen in the hotel room. I had been celibate for so long that I felt like I was a virgin again! I knew if I did not do anything intimate, it would be okay too. Giovanni was patient and understanding. There was no pressure. We had talked long and hard about this. We were not teenagers fooling around. We knew exactly what we were getting into. Despite his comment at the front desk, I knew there was no pressure.

I had packed a nice, purple, silk loungewear with a long-sleeve top and long matching pants (my idea of sexy). I put on the sleepwear after we returned to the hotel room. I walked over and sat on the edge of the bed nervously. Giovanni came over and slowly kissed me, noticing how nervous I was. He wanted to make sure *I* was sure. He took his time with me. Giovanni slowly and carefully showed me what making love truly was. I had been married twice and had never felt the fire of lovemaking until that night. Love and passion mixed with tenderness and heat. We became one, body and soul.

His experience and my inexperience helped me learn about my body. I felt like a new person. I was made to feel like a woman should in the hands of a great experienced lover. The night turned into morning as we discovered each other.

Satiated, the next morning, we walked to the wine festival—a gathering under tents in a large, open field. We were given glasses for tastings with all the vendors. I was not familiar with wine and got to sample a large variety—dry wines to very sweet wines. I discovered that day I loved wine, specifically, the sweet wines.

We returned to our hotel room to fall into each other's arms. We enjoyed every moment, learning about each other's bodies. Being with him was new and yet familiar. Giovanni bought some wine at the festival. We had a dilemma, though, that evening. We had no corkscrew, and the bar at the hotel was closed. Giovanni showed me he was a "MacGyver" by using my stiletto to uncork it. It worked!

The next day, we checked out of the hotel more of a unit than ever. Intimacy does that to people. We had taken steps to relay and cement our feelings for one another. There were no regrets. Instead, it seemed natural. His hand held mine. Promises were not made verbally, but they were understood. We knew this was it for us. Giovanni was the first boy I ever kissed when I was 11. He may well become the last man I ever kissed, too. Our lives had finally come together.

Back in New York, the second week at my parents' house was worse than the first. The boys were literally at each other's throats. My mother hollered at them to behave and yelled at me to control the boys. She made disparaging remarks to me frequently. "You can't make the boys behave. What kind of mother are you?" John disappeared from the house and refused to come home. At one point, I had to call the cops because I had no idea where he was. He didn't know anyone in New York, and he was unfamiliar with the subways and buses. The police could not locate him. John returned hours later, saying he had ridden on the subway. This was my new reality.

During the day, the boys went to their schools. After dropping off John at his school, I drove to Giovanni's apartment in the Bronx. I needed to use his computer to search for a job. I had considered using the library computers, but Giovanni's place was definitely more comfortable, and he had offered it. His one-bedroom apartment with an eat-in kitchen, living room, and office was organized and spotlessly clean. It was comfortable to work there. Giovanni was at work in the city, and I would leave by 2 p.m. to pick up John from school.

17

JOB HUNTING

I NEEDED TO MOVE OUT of my parents' house sooner than later. My work experiences and degree were in early care and education. I was interested in the following open positions: director of a childcare center or supervisor of children's programs. I polished my resume, applied for these jobs, and was called for interviews that week. The first interview was in the city. The interview went very well with the board of the childcare center. They needed someone to start immediately because their previous director had quit suddenly. They had already called my references and were impressed. I was given a tour of the facility before I made up my mind. I was appalled at the lack of books and the condition of the toys in the center. The minimal lighting in this basement setting was not ideal. In addition, the staff was not engaging with the children. One worker was on her cellphone.

I recalled the NAFCC standards and, after witnessing so many issues, I informed the board of directors that a complete revamping would be necessary for me to work there. They gave me forms to fill out, but I declined. I could not see myself working at a place like that. They were unwilling to improve the center. They did not acknowledge the problems. It was depressing.

I had two other interviews that same week. Unfortunately, the scenarios were similar. Upon entering one center, I came upon a child, crying in the middle of the room. Two staff members were in the room. One was staring out the window, and the other was on her phone. They were ignoring the weeping child on the floor. Other children were arguing in the room. I sat with the crying child, comforting them.

I turned to the staff and told them if I did take the job, they would be the first to be fired. I walked back to human resources and relayed from my quick assessment the center needed improvements, including new personnel and training sessions. The center could not afford these upgrades, which meant that they could not hire me.

The third interview was for a center in a basement of a large building—no indoor playground or gym for gross-motor play. The walls were covered with cookie-cutter art, and ditto sheets filled the children's mailboxes. In addition, the room was nearly silent. Three-year-olds were sitting quietly working on ditto sheets. One child was alone in the corner. This isolation was punishment for disrupting the class, I was told. The child had wanted to have music time and had been singing instead of sitting down quietly with his classmates.

This program subscribed to a box curriculum, and they were not willing to change it. They had a strict schedule for worksheet time that lasted over two hours in the morning. When they called to offer the job of supervisor, I declined. I felt bad for the little ones, sitting for so long, forced to do inane paperwork.

One thing I knew: I was good at childcare. I could identify a quality program, especially after going through the NAFCC accreditation process in Pennsylvania. I was desperate for a job, but did not want to be untrue to myself. The salaries offered were high and appealing (compared to Pennsylvania salaries). Yet, accepting work at these centers felt like cheating. I would be going against what I had stood for. I hit a roadblock. I could get a job, but only if I compromised my values and philosophy regarding childcare. Because I was unmasked and true to myself now, I refused to be someone I wasn't anymore. I loved myself too much now to devalue what I stood for and what I had worked for. And I would not allow myself to be boxed in, trapped in a world where I was powerless. I would strive for a career that made me proud and happy. More than money, I cared about the standards. I needed the money, but I was not going to sacrifice the standards.

I investigated a Stars program in New York and found that a pilot project called Quality Stars was starting. This program was parallel to the Keystone Stars program in Pennsylvania, except it did not offer bonuses or grants. I was very surprised this program was just created because I thought everything started in New York. Until this time, I had no idea that Pennsylvania led the way as one of the first states to promote quality, early education with its Keystone Stars program.

At home, tensions erupted October 22, 2010, a Friday night. Peter and John got into a horrible physical fight. Peter blamed John's father for all of us losing everything. John was angry with everyone and lashed back. My mother tried to break them up, and she almost got hurt in the effort. My brother warned me something needed to change; we could not keep living like this. This was my life now.

John cried and screamed that he wanted to go back to Pennsylvania. He was vehement about not wanting to live with me or be in New York any longer. It was after 11 p.m. when John called his father, and he agreed to allow John to move back with him. John was extremely angry. I had a piece of paper that could force my son to remain with me, but a custody order means nothing when your child is not happy and cannot adjust. My son was changing, and he was frequently hostile and miserable. He could not get along with his brothers at all. He hated me for moving him away from the only life he knew.

I relented. I did not see any other option. I wanted him happy. It was a Solomon decision. I had to do the best for my son. He would return to his father's house and his former school. We packed his few belongings, and I drove him back to his father's house that same night. It was a long, quiet ride with my sullen, angry son. All I could do was hope and pray that John would be safe. Only time would tell. His father had always treated him special, so I hoped it would continue.

When I dropped off my son at the house in Pennsylvania, his father greeted him. John got out of the car without saying goodbye, and he walked away without looking back at me. I could feel his hatred for me, for seemingly destroying his life. My husband smirked at me, then yelled that he had won his son back.

I drove back to New York on autopilot. I was upset to leave part of my heart in Pennsylvania. My sons were my whole life. John was my baby, and now he did not want to be with me at all.

Upon arriving at my parents' house, at nearly 4 a.m., Peter was waiting up for me. He had spoken to his father in Connecticut, and he wanted to move in with him immediately. This was sudden. Peter was told he could have his own bedroom. He could not stand the new norm for our living conditions. I felt defeated, beyond arguing. I could not force Peter to stay with me either. There was no custody order with my first husband (not that it would have mattered). Peter packed his few belongings, and we left for Connecticut.

We arrived by 6 a.m. We met his father at a local diner near his house. We needed to talk. I had not spoken to my first husband in a very long time. This was the first time we both sat down and had an amicable conversation.

Fernando is the father of my oldest two boys. Consequently, he would always be in my life in some respect. Peter had not lived with his father since we split up when he was 3.

I entrusted my son to Fernando with my blessing. We both apologized for any and all wrongdoings during our marriage. Tears were shed. We were both at fault for the ending of our relationship years earlier. I had been a child when I married him. We had not known each other well. I had married him, barely knowing him, and barely knowing myself. Since our divorce, we had moved on with our lives. He had remarried and had a beautiful, special daughter. He wished me luck with my current circumstances. He was surprised I could live with my mother for more than a week so far. (I remembered my husband had said the same thing in custody court.)

My heart was physically hurting. I had just left another piece of it in Connecticut. John and Peter had always been by my side. The decision to relocate to New York was feeling like a big mistake. I had made the difficult choice, but I had never expected my life to be torn apart. My life was over. How could I be a mother to boys who were not with me and did not want to be with me? This was heart-wrenching.

By the time I arrived at my parents' house on Saturday morning, my body was exhausted, and I was emotionally depleted. I had lost two of my boys in one night and had not slept in more than 30 hours. My mother greeted me with horrible accusations: "How could you let them leave? Don't you love them?" Added to that, she never failed to remind me: "This is what you get. You broke my heart when you moved out. This is what you deserve. Now, you know how I felt."

I had broken my mother's heart by moving out when I was barely 16. Despite leaving home, I managed to graduate in the top 10 percent of my graduating class of 300 girls. I also had earned 55 college credits and landed a full-time job. I had my own apartment with two roommates, as well. I graduated college by the time I was 20. These were no easy feats. I was proud of my accomplishments. Yet my mother thought my moving out of my parent's home was the worst thing in the world, and she continuously relayed that I had broken her heart. According to her, I deserved to feel the same pain she had.

My life was collapsing around me, and my mother was taking the opportunity to rub salt in my wounds. All I wanted was to lie down and cry. Gabriel and I talked a lot that day. He had witnessed my mother's behavior and understood how tough it was getting along with her. When I joined my parents for lunch, I found my appetite was gone. My mother insisted I eat because children were starving in Africa, and I was a horrible person for wasting good food. I could not eat. My stomach was in knots.

The following Monday, Gabriel returned to school, and I continued my job search at Giovanni's apartment. I had a dilemma. What if all my interviews went the same way and all the childcares needed upgrades they were unwilling to make? I spoke with an old client in Pennsylvania and she agreed that it would be difficult for me to find a program that operated at the high level I had achieved for years on my own. She suggested I completely switch gears and work with individual families—as a nanny or governess. I could be a modern-day Mary Poppins. I had not considered this option before, and it was well worth investigating.

It may well be that centers requiring the most intensive quality improvements are the ones that had difficulty maintaining directors. Several NAEYC-accredited centers are located in New York, but they were not hiring. (NAEYC is a NAFCC sister organization with the same code of ethics and similar quality standards except adapted for centers.) I am confident I would have been comfortable at an accredited site.

I called several agencies hiring nannies and sent them my resumes. I was hoping to get a job quickly. It was now my third week in New York without employment. My money was dwindling as I paid for gas, tolls, and food. I had spent more than half my savings to enroll John at the private school, and to cover the cost of his uniforms. That money had been wasted. I was wondering whether the price of retaining my principles and values was worth it. Why not just take the job offers? My parents certainly did not understand why I didn't. It was hard to explain.

Peter and John refused to speak to me on the phone. They ignored my phone calls. I could not speak to my husband to ask about John. I called John's old school. He had been re-enrolled. So, at least John had school—familiar territory for him. Notre Dame was a small private school with only 18 children in his grade. Sister Mary Alice, the principal, knew each child by name. She was surprised John had returned, but she assured me she would look out for him.

I felt like a failure. My self-esteem was continually battered by my mother. Sticks and stones might have felt better at this point.

Gabriel had been moved from one home where his mother got verbally harassed to another where arguments erupted all the time. I asked my father how he dealt with my mother's daily rants. He smiled slyly and turned his head to show me how he turned off his hearing aid! My dad always had a sense of humor. Great trick for him, but it couldn't work for me.

Giovanni had witnessed my mother's berating and insulting comments. He had made up his mind that he was fully in our relationship. He was committed to a life with me, so he asked me to move in with him. We had talked about a lot of things, but not living together. However, there was room in his small apartment for us. It was only two of us moving in now.

I spoke with Gabriel about moving in with Giovanni. I wanted to make sure Gabriel would be OK living with another guy. We both agreed that a move was necessary for our sanity. He wanted to make sure I was happy. I was taking a tremendous leap moving in with Giovanni.

With my father's blessing, Gabriel and I moved to Giovanni's apartment on October 30. Our entire stay at my parents' house was short. My father had given Giovanni a big hug and had asked him to treat me right.

My brother was surprised by the turn of events. He had no idea Giovanni and I had grown so close. He wanted to make sure I wasn't jumping into anything too quickly. I could not be sure of anything anymore, other than my strong feelings for Giovanni. I was still married to a man in Pennsylvania, too. Appearances were no longer an issue, though. I could not live my life thinking about what other people thought of me. I was going to be true to me.

My brother took me aside and asked me if I was sure. I was. In addition, I needed to get out of my mom's house. He invited me to come back anytime. "We have both known Gio all of our lives but living with someone is different. Are you in love with him?"

"Yes." For the first time in my life, I could say, yes. I looked happy to my brother, and I felt happy.

Giovanni's coworkers were surprised that someone he barely dated was moving in with him and bringing her son. The outside world could not understand how two people —together for less than six weeks, as far as they knew—could share an apartment. The fact is we had known each other forever.

Dating was the time when you get to know each other. Giovanni and I felt we knew each other completely because we had played as children, knew each other as teenagers and young adults. Our lives seemed destined to fall into place together. No more dating games. It was time to start our lives together.

Life in the Bronx was a real culture shock for Gabe and me. Instead of crickets at night, loud music blared from stereos of the Fordham University students, partying every night. The living room became Gabriel's bedroom. We bought a dresser for his clothes, and he slept on the futon. At least the room had a door for privacy.

Unfortunately, Gabe's commute was two hours to school every day, each way. It was his senior year, and he needed to do well. In his junior year, he had been in the National Honor Society. Now, he was barely getting by. Who could blame him? With the moves and changes, he was having a hard time adjusting. I wish he had remained in Pennsylvania, but he insisted on staying with me. He wanted to make sure I was OK. Somehow, I had raised a man who truly cared about his mother. He watched over me and observed my blooming relationship with Giovanni.

Gabriel watched Giovanni cook our meals, hold my hand and talk late into the night. We would talk everything out. Gabe noted that through his actions, Giovanni demonstrated his love for me every day. Giovanni was the first man to set a good example.

Sadly, we were forced to leave Sonny behind. Giovanni's apartment building did not allow big dogs, and Sonny, at 110 pounds, was a big dog. I hated leaving our old golden retriever behind. John had left too quickly to think to take Sonny back to Pennsylvania with him. (I thought to bring Sonny to John, but John refused to speak with me.) I worried for our dog. My mom hated him. My brother promised to care for him at my parent's house.

Giovanni asked me about opening a joint bank account with him —a big step for me, bigger than moving in with him. It meant I trusted him with my money, and he trusted me with his money. He told me very clearly he was in this for the long haul, for better or worse. This relationship was not a game for either one of us. We had both been through enough hard times to know that this was it for us. We jumped into this relationship like a person jumping into the pool—we were all in.

At Bank of America, we each got cards for joint checking and savings accounts. I was trusting him, and he was trusting me— combined finances. I was running low on funds, and he wanted to make me comfortable. I was not used to relying on anyone for money, nor did I want to. I had always worked to buy what I needed for myself and my boys. In order to make me feel more relaxed, Giovanni introduced me to his landlord and added me to the lease on his apartment.

I interviewed at nanny agencies the first week of November. I was desperate for money. I was not comfortable living with Giovanni and not pulling my financial weight. I had been the breadwinner for so many years, I knew nothing else. Since I was 16, I paid for my own rent, food, and bills without help. Now, I was depending on a man. The boys were *my* responsibility, not Giovanni's. Yet he paid for Gabriel's food and metro card, despite my opposition. His paycheck went into our new joint account, too, and I was not comfortable with only his contributions, and none from me.

Without wasting time, I continued searching for a job. Thankfully, I had several interviews with families that week. I had passed all background checks, and my references were excellent. One family hired me and wanted me to start on Nov. 9. I would be working with two children for a family in midtown Manhattan. The starting pay was much better than I had expected—four times more than I thought possible in Pennsylvania. I would be able to help financially and add money to savings. Finally, things were looking up. In less than a month, I had a job lined up and was living with Giovanni. I was very happy.

But life had a way of getting worse before it got better. In my case, I was going to learn what I was made of and become stronger than I ever thought possible.

18

CRASH, ROCK BOTTOM

IN EARLY NOVEMBER, GIOVANNI AND I went to his best friend's birthday party at a club in the city. I dressed up and got myself all made up to go out. Hair, nails, and face—all done. I took my time, too. Usually, my prepping takes about 10 minutes. This time, I spent an hour making sure my hair and face looked good. I wore tall, black, high-heeled boots, black leggings, and a loose, sexy shirt. Gabe wished us well. He stayed home, watching a movie. This was the first time since I was single that I was going out to a club in the city. Not something I was used to.

The incredibly loud music and crowded room of people—elbow to elbow—felt a bit claustrophobic. Talking over the music was impossible. Giovanni found his friend, Will, in a private area where it was roomier, and we even had seating. It was a fun night. I got to meet his best friend and other pals. I got a bit tipsy. Thankfully, Giovanni knew better than to drink because he was driving.

We left the club around 2 a.m. I laid back in my seat while we talked about the fun night. We hoped to see Will again soon. I was exhausted after the long, loud night, and I dozed off on the ride home. I awoke suddenly when my body was flung against the seat belt. My head whiplashed against the headrest. My body hurt everywhere. Something smelled dusty. I later learned it was the scent of the airbag having been deployed. Giovanni was asking me if I was OK. I could not focus enough to formulate words. I could barely stay awake. Everything was a blur.

I was taken in an ambulance to Lincoln Hospital in the Bronx where I was admitted for several days. I learned later that at a four-way intersection, a drunk driver had sped through a red light, crashing head-on into our vehicle. My car had been totaled. Because I had been asleep and slumped in the passenger seat, my seatbelt had not secured me well. The doctors informed me I had fractured the same ribs that had been broken before and my left shoulder had torn ligaments. In addition, I had a concussion and required a neck brace. The pain medications made me nauseous, causing me additional agony when I threw up. I had to do without the pain medications and deal with the pain. Luckily, Giovanni had escaped with barely a scratch.

When I was released from the hospital, the nanny job was no longer possible. There was no way I could take care of two little children. I could barely dress myself or even wash my hair. Just when I thought my life was turning around, I was literally hit and smacked down. I called my mother and told her what had happened, and she asked me what I was doing out that late at night. I explained that we were attending a birthday party. She said, "That's what happens when you go out at night." I got no support from her, and I was breaking down emotionally, too.

By December, the two-hour commute to Queens was too draining for Gabriel. He was playing hooky—this was the same person who had been on the honor roll throughout high school. He had changed. We talked at length, and we decided he should move to his father's house in Connecticut. His brother Peter was there already. He moved the first week of December. In his senior year, Gabriel wound up attending three high schools—not ideal in any sense. How I wished he had stayed in Pennsylvania to finish high school.

I was at the lowest point in my life—ROCK BOTTOM—no family, my boys no longer with me, no job possibility, no money, and a broken body. I was picked up and dropped off for physical therapy every day. Recovery was a slow, painful process. I suffered all alone in the apartment while Giovanni worked. He came home one night to find me crying uncontrollably. I cried for my boys. I barely knew them anymore. They did not call or want to answer my calls. I wept for all my losses: boys, business, and health. He let me cry myself out, then he left the room to return with the Bible. I did not want to hear anything about God. Where was God in this? How could a God allow all this to happen? He asked me to listen to him while he read from the Book of Job.

Paraphrasing what he read: Job had a wife, children, a plantation, and a home. He was a religious man. The Devil told God that Job was devout because he had wealth, family, and happiness. God disagreed. So, Satan took everything from Job to prove God wrong: wife, children, home, and plantations all were taken away. Job became horribly sick. During this ordeal, Job still held on to his faith and love for God. Because of his faith and devotion, God rewarded him tenfold. Job now had more wives and children, a bigger house, and more plantations.

After Giovanni finished his reading, I told him my faith in God was gone. There was no mustard-seed size of faith left in me. I was angry and hated God. I needed to blame someone. I shouted at Giovanni that poor Job had lost a wife he loved and no other wives would replace the first one. No number of additional children could replace the ones he lost. I saw the anguish in the story. I related at the rock-bottom level. I could not see a possibility of moving forward at all. Giovanni wanted to give me some hope, and I hollered at him. What did he know? I lost everything. My body was hurt, but I couldn't fault Giovanni for the crash. He was not to blame.

In Giovanni's apartment, I only had my clothes; everything else was his. I felt like a stranger living there. The only thing I owned was my old 1998 white Ford pickup truck. I did not want to live off a guy. I never had. I had agreed to move in with Giovanni, but I had always expected to pull my own weight. I had barely started a relationship with him, and now it was being tested.

Angela's Advice

Love is not easy or simple. It's messy and ugly, too. This is the truth. If you only see rainbows and unicorns, your relationship is not real.

GIOVANNI WAS SEEING me at my worst, and he still loved me. I had nothing to offer him, but my love, accompanied by my baggage and issues.

In the middle of December, the insurance company sent me a check for the value of the van. Financially, this check offered a small buffer for me. I had money to add to our account—finally. I bought some Christmas presents for the boys. I wanted to purchase a lot of presents and make up for my absence with gifts. I felt I needed to buy their affections, to win my children back. I was realizing, though, things mean nothing. We had lost all material possessions. Whatever they used to own meant little to them anyway. Things weren't important, but family was. We needed each other.

I remembered past Christmases in Pennsylvania when I filled the living room with so many presents there were mounds of gifts. I had believed in the commercialism of Christmas because I had bought into the picture-perfect, gift-filled room like I saw on television and in the movies. Now, all I really wanted for Christmas 2010 was to have all my boys' home with me.

Giovanni had a small tree that fit in his apartment. It would be my first year with a fake tree. He picked up my boys at their out-of-state homes. This was the first time I saw Peter and John since they moved out. They looked different and acted distant with me. They still bickered, but I also saw how much they missed each other. We played board games and watched movies. Giovanni cooked a great Italian meal on Christmas Eve.

That evening, even before the silly tokens and presents were given the next day, I felt the Christmas spirit. I looked around the small, cramped living room, crowded because we were all there: Giovanni, Gabriel, Peter, John and I plus Giovanni's sister, Pamela. It was noisy, loud, fun, and boisterous. There was friendly teasing and laughing. This was my family. My boys were, and will always mean, the world to me. That moment, that memory of family and peace, is what Christmas came to mean to me. We learned we had each other. We were still a family, even though we did not live together anymore. From the couch with my neck brace, I watched my boys, grateful for them. I may have lost everything material, but they were OK and we were together, even if it was only for Christmas.

On Christmas Day, we drove to my parents' house. It was different now with my mom. She saw my injury and noted that I was emotionally knocked down. She noticed Giovanni's affection and attention towards me. (That could not be denied.) My mom and I talked and agreed we just needed space from each other and we could get along only by living apart.

In January 2011, I was still going through physical therapy, and I felt very tired. The exhaustion forced me to rest during the day. I became very dizzy that I almost passed out at the rehab center. I was referred to a doctor who took blood samples. The results indicated that I had idiopathic aplastic anemia. The Mayo Clinic describes this disease as "a rare and serious condition." The bone marrow stopped producing new blood cells in this type of anemia, and it could cause major health issues. This diagnosis explained why I was so tired. I was out of oxygen, and my heart was working overtime. Doctors performed a bone marrow biopsy to confirm my condition. They believed I may have had it for a while, and it was now manifesting itself. I recalled how I had usually felt in Pennsylvania—very tired and cold. I had thought that was normal.

Dr. Duke—I called him that because that is where he went to school—put me on a trial drug to help alleviate the symptoms and bring up my blood counts. My ill health was consuming my life. The drugs made me feel horrible, but seemed to be working. My days were pain-filled. The side effects of nausea and hives and hair loss were continuous, but I dealt with them. My arms got bruised from all the injections and blood samples.

In early spring, Giovanni traveled to Italy to visit his parents and attend a friend's wedding. While he was away, I kept my appointments and tried to get better. On the way to the doctor one morning, I lost consciousness while driving and went off the side of the road. Luckily, I was taken to the nearest hospital, which happened to be where Dr. Duke worked. I was identified by my ID. I was admitted for several days, and I had to undergo blood and platelet transfusions. When I came to, I was all alone. No one knew I was in the hospital. Sadly, no one but Giovanni had been looking for me either, and he was in Italy. This made me realize that I really had no one by my side.

The doctors and hospital could not reach Giovanni at his parents' house in Italy because I did not have that number saved on my phone.

When I awoke in the hospital, I found out I had experienced a miscarriage. I didn't even know I had been pregnant. I was on birth control, but the medications made the birth control ineffective. I was in too much shock to be upset about the loss.

Giovanni had been calling a dead cell phone and had no idea what was going on with me. I did not have his phone number in Italy with me, so I could not call him until I was released from the hospital. The time difference and lack of numbers led to many days without any communication with Giovanni. When I got home, I rested and called Giovanni. He was beyond worried when he found out what I had been through—all alone. I called my mother and told her what had happened. She wanted me to spend the rest of the time with them while Giovanni was away. I did not want to damage our fragile relationship, so I declined.

19

WINDS OF CHANGE

I ASKED GIOVANNI TO DO one thing for me while he was in Italy. I asked him to travel to Rome and pray in St. Peter's Basilica. This church was extremely overcrowded with huge lines because of the celebration of the recent canonization of Pope John Paul II. Rome was always packed with tourists and the faithful, but, this time, more than ever. It took Giovanni three hours in line to get into the basilica, despite the guards who were moving the people along. Giovanni's sister told the guards to let him pray, and Giovanni got down on his knees and begged God to help me. He was not one to pray in a building. His praying was more private. I felt like I was at my lowest, begging God through Giovanni to help me. I rarely prayed, and now I did, with true fervor.

When I went to the doctor for follow-up blood work the next week, there was no trace of my disease. I could not believe it. The doctor could not believe it. They ran the tests again and again to make sure. I was better. I was healed—somehow, someway. My faith grew to the size of a mustard seed.

I told Giovanni about the miscarriage when he returned from Italy. He was as surprised as I was about my getting pregnant on birth control and even more startled because I was over forty and getting pregnant at that age was not always easy. Neither one of us was thinking of having children. I was done having children. My boys were growing up—two were almost adults, and John was a teenager. I did not see myself starting a family again or having a child with yet another man. Marriage was not something we talked about either because I was still married.

My health was finally good. I needed regular check-ups, but I was given a clean bill of health. Consequently, I started my job search again. I went through nanny agencies to get hired. There were three families that wanted to hire me. One was in the city with one child. The con was the location in the city and very long hours, but the pro was the salary— the highest pay of the three offers. The second family was in Scarsdale. The con was the atmosphere—the house was like a museum, the kids were expected to stay clean, and lots of activities were planned. The pro was the close commute. The third family's pros were a close, 10-minute commute, one child with one on the way and a laid-back, down-to-earth family. No cons to this job, so I took this wonderful position as a nanny for an incredible family. They treated me like one of the family. I loved every minute of caring for their child and later, their children. Both boys and I would go hiking, to museums, to parks, to pools, and to story times at libraries. We traveled every day, and I loved it.

During this time, my brother called to tell me that Sonny, our wonderful dog, had a nosebleed that would not stop. He took him to the vet, and Sonny was diagnosed with a brain bleed. I had no choice but to order the doctor to put him to sleep. I recalled all the great times with this wonderful dog. Sonny brought happiness to our lives. I was sorry I could not be there for him at the end. I called John to tell him the sad news. He was very upset and blamed my mother for injuring Sonny and not noticing he had been bleeding from his brain.

In June 2011, John called to tell me he was at his best friend's house because his father had been taken into the psych ward. John had come home from school and found his father unresponsive in his bed with partly empty Percocet and Ativan bottles next to him. John performed CPR and called the paramedics. They took his father away in an ambulance, and John called his best friend to pick him up. John then finally told me the truth of what had been going on since October of the previous year with his father.

My ex's life had changed. His father had received a settlement from an insurance company, and that had allowed them some financial freedom, but despite that, they lived off dollar-store food because they could not afford much. At two points during the year, the electric company had shut off the electricity but, because of my husband's health issues, Con Ed was forced by law to turn it on again. The water pump had broken, and his father could not afford to fix it. They used the neighbor's hose to get water into the house! They connected several hoses to get across both properties. His father demanded that John help him, like the nurses used to care for him. John had to be at his father's beck and call. His father could have had his nurses come back to help him but chose to have John work nurse duty.

I could not believe I had been kept in the dark about these details. I had been under the false assumption everything was OK, not great, but at least OK. When I visited John in Pennsylvania on the weekends, he seemed alright. While I was injured from the accident and then suffering with illness, I had not been able to make trips to Pennsylvania. That's when things got worse for John. He was always quiet, and he kept things to himself. He had been put in a situation that was beyond his young years. He had become very bitter toward his father. John agreed to move to the Bronx with me. He would make the living room his bedroom, just like Gabriel had before him. He was not happy about coming to New York, but was not fighting me about it either.

I needed to go back to court to get custody because John was still a minor. The court looked at the facts and again granted me full custody. My husband tried to fight this order, but his mental health was questioned, and his appeal was denied.

We went to my parents' house to celebrate Father's Day in June. The older boys were with their father, so it was just Giovanni, John, and me at the cookout. Giovanni barbecued for the gathering, and we each enjoyed a good meal. My mother had always been a firm believer that people should not live together if they were not married. I seemed to be an exception to her rule because she said, "God understands your situation!" I laughed at the thought.

My father and I had an interesting discussion that day. He wanted to know when Giovanni and I were going to buy a house!

"How can we," I asked my dad. We had been together barely a year.

His response was simple: "Como? You love him. You are with him and want a future together. Buy a house."

Our conversation stayed with me, and Giovanni and I started talking about the possibility.

The down payment was an issue. We were not in a financial position to do anything to make this dream possible. My parents and Giovanni's parents wanted to help us out, and they gifted us the money for a down payment on a house. They knew how hard our lives had been, and this was their way of helping us begin again. My brother chipped in, as well, for the down payment. We were extremely thankful and grateful for their generosity. It was understood that with these gifts, they were granting us their blessings.

We now just needed to find a house to make our home. Barely a year ago, I was living in Pennsylvania and closing my business and walking away from a house. Now, I was house hunting with Giovanni, my partner.

Buying a house proved to be a long and hard undertaking. We wanted to live in a nice neighborhood with low taxes and a close commute to the city. The house also needed bedrooms for all of my boys—that was a major goal. "Build it, and they will come." I sought a two-family home with separate entrances.

We discussed opening a childcare. This was my dream, but I knew it would be very hard to do in New York. But with a two-family home, we could bring in extra income by renting out one floor if we needed to.

Our real estate agent, Dave, worked diligently to show us many possibilities. Every weekend, we traveled to Westchester County to see possible houses. Some were absolutely gorgeous, but there was always something wrong. For example, a beautiful house with a picket fence was gorgeous from the outside, but when we walked through the house, we found shackles, handcuffs and a whip on the floor in the corner of the basement. None of us knew what to say. I gripped Giovanni's arm hard. I wanted to run out. As we walked upstairs, we saw nude paintings along the walls. One of the bedrooms had mirrors all around and on the ceiling with a circular bed in the center. There was a dressing room filled with costumes: maid, nurse, doctor, and so forth. I walked past an office where a woman was receiving cash from a guy. We left this house, knowing full well there was no way I could live in a former whorehouse. Dave did not need to ask us our opinion of the house.

Other homes we visited had no backyards. Still, others were located near gas stations or completely inaccessible to main roads. Others were beautiful, but way out of our budget or too small, like a dollhouse with no room for any possibilities. It was disheartening to house hunt.

After I moved to New York, I grew close to another family friend, Jack. He became something like a girlfriend to me, my go-to person. We had all grown up together. He was Giovanni's mother's cousin, which made him Giovanni's second cousin. Jack's mother used to be my mother's best friend, as well. Jack's older two boys were just a year older than Gabriel and Peter. Jack also had been involved in several relationships, so he understood the hardships and societal stigmas associated with having had multiple marriages and children with different mothers.

Coincidentally, Jack and I were both going through divorce, custody, and child support hearings. Our court dates were within days of each other, so we had a lot to talk about, and we counseled each other. Jack lived in Florida, so our relationship grew strong through numerous phone conversations. It was nice to have another ear to listen to me and offer support. Jack encouraged me, cheered me on, and advised me. He was always just a phone call away. We spoke honestly to each other, too. The boys understood Jack was like a girlfriend, and Giovanni respected our relationship. He understood we had a platonic friendship. He accepted that Jack could relate to a part of my life that he could not. (I found out later that when I was in the hospital with idiopathic anemia, Jack was frantic, looking for me, too.)

From 2011 to 2014, I was in court every three to four months. My husband wanted to fight about custody, although John refused to see him. I had to argue with John and force him to see his father, or else I would be held in contempt of court. I would drive John to the exchange spot in New Jersey, and he would refuse to get out of the car or run away. I tried telling this to the court, but the judge still demanded that John spend time with his father. My husband wanted support from me, and the Court granted him alimony because I had always been the breadwinner. I started paying my him more than half my weekly salary. My paychecks were going to my husband once I started working as a nanny.

It was an uphill fight every time we traveled to Pennsylvania. My husband was still fighting the PFA, stating the same, tired argument that it had been granted without his presence. He even dragged my parents and brother into court with subpoenas in an effort to dismiss the PFA. Instead of dismissal, the order was made permanent.

Jack understood the ins and outs of the court system as much as I did because we both had been through civil court several times. Our war stories were comparable. Though Giovanni was my partner, he could not understand what I was going through with my husband. His divorces had been amicable. There had never been children involved or support hearings. I leaned on Jack through this hard time, calling him constantly. He would call me endlessly with his issues, too. Thankfully, I had unlimited minutes on my cell phone.

Giovanni and I had such a long history before becoming involved; when my aunt and uncle, Giovanni's godparents, found out we were together, they were very happy for us. We traveled to visit family a lot. Our relatives said we should have gotten together when we were in our 20s, instead of marrying other people. However, I knew an early marriage with Giovanni would never have worked out. We would have been too immature. Besides, I would never have had my three wonderful boys. We both needed to grow up and experience life before coming full circle back to each other.

My extended family never knew about my private life. While I was married to my second husband, I lost all contact with them. Now, with Giovanni, I regained my family. I saw my cousins, Elizabeth and Carmen, after so many years. I met their children for the first time. I looked forward to traveling to Long Island to visit my Tia Rosa and Tio Rafael. I thought of them as my second parents. I loved my Tia's cooking. I was not lonely anymore.

After three months of house hunting, Giovanni and I told our real estate agent we were finished. We felt like we were wasting our time. Dave asked to drive us to one last house that had just gone on the market. We agreed only because it was on the way back home. Giovanni and I pulled up to a strange sight. A gazebo was at the start of a long, long entryway. I didn't even want to get out of the car; it was so different. It did not look like a house. I found out later the covered entryway was more than 80 feet long. It had been built as a cable car house in the 1800s. I walked in, ahead of Giovanni, through the first floor with the owner next to me. I immediately saw the possibilities on that floor. My imagination raced beyond the old-fashioned house. A small foyer led to the kitchen on one side and to the dining area (art room and eating area) on the other side. That room opened into a large, open space with tall ceilings (block and music areas with the piano in front of the fireplace). A bedroom could be an office and attached to it was the first bathroom (nice and big). Next, there was a hallway to three different rooms in the back of the house. I defined these rooms in my mind as the science room (porcelain tile, perfect for spills and messes), dramatic play, and literacy (built-in mirrors on the doors). There was another bathroom and a third room that could be a children's gym/ball-pit space. My mind was spinning with the possibilities. I was picturing everything in my head. I was smiling and clapping like a little girl.

This house was clearly what I was looking for. As we walked through the house, I told the owner my plans. My excitement overflowed. I did not hide that I loved it. This was it. Giovanni was hesitant. He did not see what I was seeing. His perspective was this: an old house, too much work to put into it, in need of expensive upgrades and a very strange set-up. It was true the house needed a lot of work—upgraded windows, roof, boiler, floors, walls, you name it. Upgrades had not been completed in 20 years or more. Even the yards were overgrown and could not be walked through. The only decent floor was the main floor that could be a childcare space. The house featured three other living space floors. The home needed so much work, much more than just a little painting and spackling. Yet, I knew this was it.

My brother called to ask how the house hunting had gone. I told him what we had found. He asked when we were putting in a bid. Jack and I spoke, too, and he was happy we had found a house that could work for us. Giovanni and I talked late into the night, listing the pros and cons. I pushed for the house. This was it. We put in a bid the following morning. The owner accepted our bid, and we were on our way to home ownership.

Giovanni had a conversation with the homeowner, Elaine. Her

parents were from the same region in Italy as Giovanni's father. Coincidentally, they discovered they had the same acquaintances.

We hired a previous client of mine from Pennsylvania, a real-estate attorney named Lorrie, to help us with the house purchase. Ariel, her daughter, had been one of my first childcare children, and she and my boys attended the same private school while growing up. Lorrie was happy to see my life had improved, and I was doing better than ever.

During the months while the loans and paperwork were going through, I'd stop by the house to check it. I was very excited about starting over. One day, while I was visiting our new home, a stray cat approached me, then rubbed itself on me. The cat walked with me to the side door and entered the property with me. A neighbor dropped by and introduced himself. He noted the cat and said my cat behaved like a dog. I said the cat wasn't mine.

The neighbor did not recognize the cat. Before I departed, I rubbed the cat goodbye and I turned to get in my truck. The cat jumped into the truck ahead of me and sat down on the front seat. I tried getting the cat out, but he jumped in the back of the truck, making himself comfortable there. I walked door to door around the block asking if someone was missing a cat. No one recognized the cat. He had planted himself in my truck. We adopted the cat (or he adopted us) and named him August because that was the month he found us and joined our family. August moved into the Bronx apartment and became our first pet together.

The final contract on the house was signed December 16, 2011. At the suggestion and advice of a lawyer friend, we did not put my name on the mortgage. I was still married and he could fight for part-ownership of this house. I needed to wait another year before I could file for a divorce in New York. My brother and Giovanni became owners of the house until I could safely add my name to the deed. This would prove to be a great decision.

20

STARTING MY DREAM AGAIN

THE NIGHT WE SIGNED THE paperwork, Giovanni picked me up and carried me over the threshold of our new home as if we had just gotten married. We went up to the terrace that overlooks the Hudson River and watched the sunset on the Palisades. Giovanni and I toasted our wonderful luck and life together in our new home. We looked forward to a new future. That same weekend, we began the move-in process. We didn't have money for renovations or remodeling; we just moved in. This was right before Christmas, and I wanted at least a tree for the boys in the new house. The house was our Christmas gift to them. John chose his bedroom and game room. Gabriel and Peter were still living in Connecticut with their father. I was hoping that now— with the large home (4,300 square feet)—they would want to move in with me. Only time would only tell.

Gabriel and Peter visited from Connecticut. They were surprised with the unique setup of the four-story home. Giovanni invited everyone to play hide-and-seek in the dark. The boys were all for it. Because the house was barely furnished (Giovanni's furniture from the Bronx apartment only filled three rooms in the house), the tubs and closets were used as hideouts. The house echoed with happy shrieks when the seeker found the hiders. The boys played, laughed, and scared each other and us late into the night. We used our cellphones as flashlights to get around in the dark. New memories were being formed, and the house was becoming a home.

I explained my new plans to my employer, and we were all sad to say our goodbyes. This family had helped me so much, and I had grown very fond of their boys. Working five days a week, more than 11 hours a day with two children made the work personal. I had become a major adult role model in their children's lives. The mom helped me set up a website for my new business. We worked together many nights, long after the boys were asleep and she was tired. I helped the family train another nanny to replace me. My last day with this amazing family was in January 2012.

This was really going to happen. I experienced a lot of emotions: fear, happiness, anxiety, and hopefulness. I felt like a little kid on Christmas morning. I was opening a childcare again. I never thought this was possible, especially when, just 15 months earlier, I had lost everything and had hit rock bottom. Job's story from the Bible came back to haunt me in a good way. I was reminded that dreams can come true.

In January 2012, we emptied the storage area in Pennsylvania. A couple of my previous clients, Kristen and Joy, were happy to see me again and came to help. I was happy to see familiar faces. They both noted I looked content, and I was. Giovanni made me happy but, most importantly, I was happy. When we opened the storage unit, all the wonderful memories poured out. Each box of toys, books, and supplies had a story. It took a couple hours to load everything. After everything was loaded into the U-Haul, we said our final goodbyes to our wonderful friends and Pennsylvania.

I applied for my childcare license and submitted all my paperwork. I would file my business as an LLC under Giovanni's name to protect it from my husband. (As a corporation, it would be harder, if not impossible, for him to gain part-ownership.) I needed to be protected. Every time I saw my ex during custody exchanges, he would shout disparaging, hurtful remarks at me, reminding me that I was still married to him, that I belonged to him.

While I waited for approval from the state, I unpacked, arranged, rearranged, cleaned, painted, repaired, and organized the childcare floor. I pulled all-nighters. Jack helped me formulate my business plan and outlook because he had been a business owner several times. Projections were written and revised with Jack's assistance.

I set up the childcare floor as I had envisioned it during my first visit to the house. I got 12 lockers on Craigslist for the class. I placed them in the foyer. I made a bulletin board for special notes in the entryway; I was hoping to hang the monthly calendars and menus there, as well. I bought two tables with 16 small chairs and placed them in the art/eating area. I filled the art rack with paper and supplies (crayons, markers, pencils, stencils, magazines, scissors, hole punchers, stampers, tape, etc.) and recyclables. I bought mailboxes for each child's home notes and artwork. I painted a wall with chalkboard paint and had a bin with chalk for the children. I unpacked easels and an art rack, too. The main room featured the piano blocking the fireplace, just like I had visualized the first day I saw our home.

This became a home. My home. Our family house. This feeling was new and wonderful. This home was not going to be taken from me. It was more than bricks or mortar. This house was filled with love.

I placed the music center shelves next to the piano. The more delicate and noisy instruments I placed on higher shelves, so they could only be used with supervision. This main room also became the block room. I filled a shelf with wooden blocks, cardboard blocks, Legos, magnetics, small-people cars, and other fine-motor toys. I placed a magnetic wall on one side and used ramps and balls for that section. On another wall, I made a felt board and put felt pieces in a basket for the class to play with. I had puzzles sorted for all different age groups. I placed a block table in the corner for the train set and games, as well.

The science room took time. Giovanni helped me set up his fish tank there. He spent time adding fish and building a beautiful environment for them. Guinea pigs were comfortable in a large habitat. Worms also enjoyed a nice dirt container. The science shelves were filled with different nature items (pinecones, river stones, sticks, leaves, real beehives, real bird nests). I also bought a large water table and a sensory table, and each could accommodate six children. Magnifying glasses, microscope, John's pinned specimens from his entomology class, science books, tweezers, measuring cups, and spoons were all placed throughout the room. I bought a large wind tunnel for the class to explore wind and gravity. I also purchased a light cube for clear magnetics, X-rays, and sand.

The books in the literacy room were sorted. I labeled sections of the library shelves for the different genres: emotions, special needs, Spanish, Italian, school-age books, and preschool books. Board books were placed in baskets by the floor mat. I used pillows to make a comfy area for reading. I took out all the puppets and put them on stands and in bins. The puppet theater was placed next to the puppets. I bought a closet with hanging space and drawers for the dramatic play area and filled it with assorted costumes—from community helpers to ethnic outfits.

I had a much larger space for my childcare than in Pennsylvania. Previously, I had only wished for certain supplies, but now, with so much room, I was able to purchase them. In time, I even got a giant Lite-Brite for the literacy room. The colorful pegs were great for small hands. I had seen one at a local children's museum and knew I had to have something like that for my class. Luckily, a grant helped me buy it.

Last of all, I converted the final room on the childcare floor into a children's gym. I covered the floor with soft gym mats, bought a large 8-foot soft ball pit, soft balance beam, soft blocks, and a large mirror with padding. The space was perfect for jumping, somersaulting, and having fun. It became the highlight of tours during interviews. Children needed a place to "shake their sillies out." This gym was ideal for that.

Outside, I converted the dark and dreary entryway into a welcoming, fun space. I hung signs on the beams, painted a wooden alphabet and numbers in bright colors, and placed them along the entryway. I hung a wooden Pooh Bear and his friends on the entry beams, too.

Eventually, I purchased a three-child carousel and placed it in the gazebo at the entrance. John made a small bench for parents, and he also built wooden planters as decorations. The entryway became eye-catching and appealing. I also ordered a banner to display the name of the business.

Three outdoor play areas were created. One was the standard playground: a low slide and climber, chimes, and sandbox. Balls, hoops, and ride-on toys were on this level. The second level was my nature playscape yard with a sensory garden (mint and herbs, wind-chimes, fake flowers and worms). I made a reading corner under a trellis with two chairs and books in a covered bin. I formed an outdoor musical board with pots and pans. Giovanni made a mud kitchen using an old, small oven. I had real kitchen tools placed there for the class to play with. I had a handyman cut up a log as a balance beam and another log as seating stumps or stepping stones. The third level became the garden area. I had to have a garden again. I wanted to bring nature to the class. I missed that from Pennsylvania. We added a greenhouse and a compost bin later with grant money.

All was ready and in order. State inspectors and the fire marshal came and reported no issues, and I received my license in February 2012!

It wasn't that simple to get started, though. I waited for months to get clients—six months to be exact. Advertising took time. I placed flyers on cars, dropped off business cards at local businesses, and handed out flyers at parades. I paid for Google and Yelp ads. I sponsored baseball teams to get my name out. In addition, ads were placed in my church bulletin and in the local paper. It was exhausting and very costly. Still, no one called. I contacted other neighborhood providers to meet them, but they refused to meet me, thinking that I would steal their clients. I started wondering whether it was ever going to happen. But I was not going to give up. Giovanni was the only one bringing in an income at that time.

While waiting for clients to call and sign up, I worked on updating my family handbook, reviewing contracts and agreements, consent forms for activities, a termination policy, emergency plans, a medical policy, behavior management documents, and napping consent forms. I made files, printed the necessary paperwork, and created packets.

The rooms looked great. Every day, I checked the rooms and straightened and fluffed the already fluffed-up pillows. I was not giving up on my dream. I was so close now. I would go over lesson plans and review curriculum ideas in my office. I set up folders and bins for the different months and topics. I readied folders with the application packet, hoping for clients. I kept myself very busy.

Finally, I got my first phone call in August. I had an interview with a follow-through sign- up. Ayden was the first child in my care for three weeks. Then I received a phone call from my previous employer. They had gone through three nannies after I had left them in January that year. It had not worked out with any nanny after I left, and they wanted to work with me again. They wanted to enroll the boys into my program. This would be a huge change for them because they were used to having someone in their home. Now Michael and William were brought to my childcare in the mornings. I was more than happy to have these boys again. Our relationship changed. I was their teacher, not their nanny. I would not be taking the boys on day trips, but instead, I would be planning lessons and learning activities. Their parents had to follow my family handbook and policies. Our relationship evolved with no hitches.

Over the years, my relationship with this family grew into a friendship that I hold dear. When their children were no longer in my care, we remained in touch. And we still are. I take their boys on day trips when I am able, such as museums and amusement parks. During summers, my whole family is invited to go to their lake house where we canoe and water ski.

After I enrolled Michael and William, I slowly enrolled other clients until I had a waiting list. As a group family provider, I needed an assistant listed on my license. The plan was for Gabriel to work with me. He had decided to move back with me since he had finished high school in Connecticut. Unfortunately, because I did not get clients until August and I was not at capacity to need an assistant until January, he wound up getting another job locally.

In December 2012, Peter moved in with us, too. All my boys were now under one roof. It had taken two long, hard years apart, but we were all together again. Miracles did happen. We got to know each other again as a family. I appreciated my boys more now than ever and was very grateful they wanted to live with me.

That Christmas was special. It was not about presents anymore. It was about us and building memories. Big meals—all together as a family—were becoming traditions for these occasions. We went into the city and ice skated in Central Park. We walked through Rockefeller Center and took in all the beautiful sights of the holidays. We watched street performers and carolers, too. It was cold, but fun. Good memories with my family were all I wanted. I realized how precious and priceless memories could be.

21

LIFE WITH GIOVANNI

GIOVANNI HAD A FAMILY OVERNIGHT. The noise and rowdiness grew on him. The fact that the boys were not very neat or organized was something he learned to live with. He accepted the mess and noise in exchange for a large family by his side. The boys learned to keep the common areas of the house clean. Their bedrooms were their own business. Giovanni remembered his quiet, organized, clean, empty apartment before he got together with me, and he did not miss it.

The boys accepted Giovanni as their stepfather with no issues, and they also considered him a role model. They respected him, and he respected them. There was a mutual appreciation. The boys could turn to Giovanni for advice, and they genuinely liked being around him. They had known him for so much of their lives, and the shift in their relationship occurred naturally.

One weekend I found Giovanni quietly resting on our bed. I asked him if something was wrong. He told me his life had changed so much, and he was just grateful. We both were grateful. Happy tears were shed among kisses. We had found each other when the time had been right. Our lives had improved because of each other. It was a solemn moment for us, and we acknowledged how much we meant to each other. Our love and strength had gotten us this far.

We talked a lot that afternoon. The one thing missing in Giovanni's life was a child of his own. In his previous marriages, he had never been blessed with a child. He loved my boys and was grateful for them. He wanted, though, to have someone to raise and love as his own. We talked about conceiving a child. It would be starting over for me with a newborn. I knew how hard the newborn stage was, and I was not looking forward to it: sleepless nights, long breastfeeding sessions, and diapers. Despite all the tireless work, I was willing. So, Giovanni and I decided to try and conceive a child.

In the meantime, Peter did not have a job yet, and we discussed the idea of him working with me in the childcare. Peter went through the process of becoming my assistant, and he was approved. He proved to be my right hand and a steadfast partner for my business. We balanced each other perfectly. He was the fun, rowdy one, and I was the serious, meticulous one. He brought a new aspect to the work, and the children loved him instantly. He had always been a child magnet, and he innately knew what to do with children. He had always been the most animated and excited of my boys with the class in Pennsylvania, too.

I would plan a painting lesson, and Peter would have the class paint on the table instead of paper. I would talk about worms, and Peter would go worm hunting with the class. He always went the extra mile with the children. Peter reminded me of his younger self, back when he assisted me in Pennsylvania. I had flashbacks of Peter reading to the class as a child himself. Now, he was a young adult, reading the same books in our new childcare.

I loved every moment working with Peter. I trusted that the children were in great hands with him. Some parents took time to warm up to Peter—a male, working in early childhood—but, after getting to know Peter, they were won over. (There is a stigma regarding men working with young children, making this business mostly a woman's world. This perception is hard to change. It is assumed that men are not nurturing or as loving as women. It is also thought that men should not change a girl's diaper for fear of abuse.)

Peter earned his associate's degree in child development and he was the only male in class. He attended many local conferences and workshops, too. He found out he was the sole male unless you counted the keynote speakers. Despite these struggles, Peter remained my right- hand worker, following my lead.

Peter and I needed to hire another full-time worker. Finding the right person was not easy. We went through countless resumes and interviews. I would hire someone who, on paper, looked good, and then we would find out we were not compatible at all. I had trouble with staff members who were chronically late and unreliable. Others would not respect my policies. Dress code could be an issue, too. Ethics came into question with others.

In one instance, I had a new child in the program, and he was having a hard time adjusting. He was 4, and he constantly cried for his mother. It was his first experience away from her, so he was suffering from severe separation anxiety. With patience, respect, understanding, time, and love, children learn to be comfortable in their new environment. When this child pleaded, "I want my mom," the new staff member, who was on probation, said, "Me, too, so you go home, and I get some peace and quiet!" No one should speak to a child like that. She was heartless.

I now understood the high turnover in childcare staff. I went through seven workers in five years. Our goal was accreditation with trained staff. I kept interviewing and training assistants.

While I moved forward, ensuring quality childcare in my work, I had personal and private challenges to deal with. Giovanni and I had decided we wanted to conceive a child. I had gone to the doctor and was told that I should be able to conceive with no issues. No in vitro fertilization (IVF) was necessary. So, we tried. Unfortunately, I miscarried—again and again and again. The losses were devastating. No one could figure out why I couldn't stay pregnant.

In August 2013, I was pregnant for the fifth time. I was at 20 weeks. Sonograms showed a healthy baby. The fetus had a strong and typically fast heartbeat. I moved into my mom's house during the summer break because our home's windows were being replaced, and the dust was too much for me. One day at my mother's home, I started cramping. I called Giovanni. We both knew what was happening, and there was nothing we could do to stop it. My body rejected every pregnancy.

We went to the obstetrician, and she confirmed what we already knew. I was miscarrying, and there was nothing anyone could do—five miscarriages. They allowed me time to cry for our loss by giving us privacy in the office. The doctor spoke to Giovanni and told him we should stop trying at this point. She recommended I speak with a therapist. I was devastated. I just wanted to lay in bed and cry. The loss of our child broke my heart. I didn't even want to talk to Jack when he called. Jack spoke with Giovanni and told him what I needed was a change in scenery and lots of TLC. He suggested Giovanni and I go away for the weekend to a bed-and-breakfast.

We did. Giovanni drove me to Warwick, N.Y., where Jack had lived many years earlier. The Victorian bed-and-breakfast was beautifully old fashioned. We walked around the town of Warwick and discovered the vineyards. We ate at homey, intimate, hole-in-the-wall restaurants. The four-poster bed and fireplace in the bedroom at the inn made me feel like I was in England. We cuddled each other in that big bed. We were both grieving the loss. I came back from that getaway refreshed and calm.

Giovanni and I had accepted we were not going to have biological children. Although the boys called Giovanni their stepfather, he still wanted to raise a child of his own. We looked into adopting a child. By December 2013, we had scheduled a meeting with an adoption agency and began the approval process—it was going to be a long road. There were a few choices: national, international, or fostering. After much discussion, we decided to adopt from Colombia because of our shared heritage. Giovanni's mom and both of my parents are from Colombia.

In January 2014, I had my final court date for my divorce. A lawyer from PACE Women's Justice Center, who specialized in abuse cases, had taken my case based on the domestic violence and emotional abuse that I had suffered. The case had been filed in a White Plains court. My husband came to court and refused to sign off on the divorce. First, he asked for $100,000. My lawyer told me that even if I had that cash, there was no way he was going to get that. Then, he stated he still loved me, and I belonged to him. He argued that I needed to care for him. He complained, his voice quivering and eyes tearing, that the house was empty, life was not the same without me, and he wanted me to come back with the boys.

My lawyer told the court exactly how it had been with him and that my husband was painting a very different picture from reality. She described the years of emotional abuse and malicious manipulations. She did not hold back at all. The judge asked me to confirm the details.

I did. In hindsight, my life with my husband had been torturous. I had been forced to live a double life. Superficially, it always seemed fine, but, in reality, I hid the pain and hurt every day.

Now that I was with Giovanni, my life was so different. I did not want to ever feel that oppressed again. I was now a new person. I was free to be me. I was free to speak my mind without getting scared of loud, vicious reproach. The boys now enjoyed a peaceful household, too.

My husband wanted the items I had taken from the house returned to him. He wanted all the childcare materials, arguing they belonged to him. He claimed it was his business that I closed down. He demanded that I return all the New York Yankees mementos, as well. I refused. I had left him the house and all the furniture, including the boys' bedroom furnishings—valuable properties.

The judge, thankfully, appreciated my point of view and advised my husband that since I had left him all furnishings, he was not entitled to mementos, as well. The judge did not even address his demand for the childcare items because he had never operated, nor could he ever run the childcare because of his health.

My husband's next tactic was to tell the court he was owed half of my current childcare business in New York and part ownership of the new house since it was marital property. I was ready for this claim and presented documents to prove these properties were not in my name. I was grateful that nothing was under my name. He had not expected this disclosure, and he cursed me and pounded the table. His surprise at this turn of events was palpable. He couldn't take ownership of anything that was not in my name. We had to take a recess while he was taken out and calmed down. My lawyer and the judge saw my husband for what he really was.

I needed this divorce over. When my lawyer told me my husband was willing to settle for $1,000, I was happy. This would be the last alimony payment to him. It was finally over. After four years in New York, I was awarded a final divorce decree, and my ties to Pennsylvania were severed completely.

My ex later tried to appeal the divorce, but was denied. He was officially my ex-husband. I was wholly free from him. That was the last time I ever saw him or heard from him. The PFA would remain in effect permanently.

22

SUNSHINE

I WAS ON BIRTH-CONTROL PILLS because we had decided we were no longer going to try for a baby. I couldn't go through another devastating miscarriage. We were choosing a birth mother and reviewing adoption files. Birth control is 99 percent effective, but that decreases when the pills are not taken properly. I did not realize my pet bird, a conure named Sunshine, had gotten into my pills. I assumed I had taken my pill for the day because it was missing; I had, in fact, not taken it. This bird spent time with me in my bedroom every evening. I had adopted him as a baby and fed him baby food for several weeks. He was affectionate with me. He also played with the pills on my nightstand without me noticing.

So, I had missed doses. In January, Giovanni and I had an appointment with a specialist. I had been referred to him after my last miscarriage to make sure that there were no underlying issues with my uterus. At the doctor's office, we were completely blindsided—I was pregnant. I couldn't go through the loss of another baby again. I wept because this was not great news. The doctor immediately ran tests and determined I had a condition that could only diagnosed during pregnancy. (No other doctor had looked for this condition.) It restricted the blood flow to the placenta, causing the fetus to die in utero.

The doctor calmed me down because I was visibly upset with this news. I was hyperventilating and needed to breathe into a bag. He told me I needed Lovenox shots twice daily to aid the blood flow into the placenta. The shots were painful, but Giovanni discovered that when he iced the area to numb the skin, the pain decreased. I was fearful I could lose the baby, but I tried to stay hopeful. The doctor's diagnosis made sense. I was now giving my baby a fighting chance to live. All my boys had been born prematurely, and the doctor believed that because my uterus was misshapen, the pregnancies couldn't come to full term.

One night, while cuddling with Giovanni, I told him I felt sad for our baby. He didn't understand what I meant. I told him although the baby would have siblings, they would be so much older that he or she would grow up as an only child. He said it was okay because he or she could play with the children in the childcare. But I knew it wasn't the going to be the same. The child would be alone on nights and weekends. We both agreed, but there was no way we would try to have a second child after this pregnancy. (I had already considered having my tubes tied after this pregnancy.)

The following month, I had to go to the emergency room with severe, nonstop morning sickness or hyperemesis gravidarum (HG, the same type of morning sickness that Kate Middleton suffered). My HCL hormone levels did not correspond with the length of my pregnancy. The nausea was the worst feeling. I just planted myself next to the toilet bowl. The doctor ran an ultrasound and gave me a pill to help with the nausea. I did not want to take anything for it. I was worried about side effects for my baby.

There was really nothing the doctors could do for me because I refused the medicine. Despite the HG, the pregnancy was OK. Interestingly, I learned later the pill I was offered was featured on a commercial by a law firm, gathering clients for a lawsuit. (If you had taken this medicine and had experienced certain symptoms, then call this law office.) Thankfully, I had never taken the medication.

On the drive home, my obstetrician called me with an update regarding my ultrasound and blood work. He offered congratulations on being pregnant with twins! I almost crashed the car and went off the road with to his announcement. Twins.

How? What? Because my bird chewed through the pills and I did not take them correctly, I hyper-ovulated two eggs. The mistake in birth control worked like Clomid in me. Clomid is used by fertility specialists to help women get pregnant. So, the week prior, I had told Giovanni I was sad for our only child growing up alone and the Universe/God/Fate had heard my comment and gave me twins! Someone was laughing at this irony. Not me. I drove the rest of the way home in a daze. I have no idea how I got home. Giovanni had just arrived home when I pulled into my parking spot. I couldn't risk telling him right on the street and making a scene.

I told him we needed to talk. It felt like an out of body experience. Giovanni sat down on our bed. He clearly expected to hear I was miscarrying again. His face said it all. I was in shock with the news, so I looked completely blank. I explained that I was expecting twins. He cried and laughed. We called our families with the news. The boys were ecstatic.

My family treated me like I was a porcelain doll, knowing quite well what was at stake.

A twin pregnancy, being over 40, and having a history of multiple miscarriages put me in an even higher risk category. I visited the doctor weekly during the first trimester, and I continued taking Lovenox shots twice daily. I continued to work with my class while Peter assumed a stronger lead role. The doctor wrote orders for a visiting nurse (Shelley) to weekly administer progesterone shots. Shelley supported me throughout my entire pregnancy. The doctor was very hands-on and knowledgeable about my condition, and he helped calm my fears with his positive energy.

At 12 weeks, I graduated to another specialty obstetrician because my current doctor specialized in the first term only. Unfortunately, the start of my second trimester was riddled with problems. I had severe cramping twice and went to the hospital, expecting the worse. The doctor was paged and never called back. The second time I was in the hospital, the staff said the doctor would see me the next day.

I made an appointment to see her. Later, I learned the doctor had not realized I was in the hospital previously. I shared with her my fear of losing the twins. Her response: "You're still pregnant, aren't you?" She was dismissive and callous. I needed to find a specialist who would truly support me through this pregnancy. In the meantime, I had to continue with this cold, uncaring professional.

I would go for an ultrasound, and the tech would do it. The doctor would see me in her office and speak to me while looking at her computer. There was no personal touch. She never examined me. Only techs and nurses from her practice were hands-on with me.

My insurance was limited. Giovanni and I spoke at length about the situation, and we agreed his insurance offered much better coverage than mine. We discussed getting married. Although I was single and free, I was not mentally prepared for this step. It wasn't that I didn't love Giovanni, but the marriage would be my third—our third marriage. It could provoke ridicule because of a societal stigma. I needed to mentally get over that hump. It also felt wrong to get married while I was pregnant—better before or after. (Maybe I was still somewhat of a traditionalist.)

Jack talked to me and helped me sort out my feelings. It was a big step. I had gotten married too young the first time. The second time, I had avoided the warning signs. Now, I was older, hopefully wiser, and marriage had new meaning. Everything about my relationship with Giovanni had been unconventional and completely unexpected. We never really dated, except for two times. Giovanni and I moved in together within two months of starting our relationship. We bought a house a little over a year later. We established a childcare business shortly after buying the house. Our relationship had moved at lightning speed, and in our four years together, we had lived through some seriously tough times.

I was also in love with Giovanni, and he loved me. Both of us had proven our love for each other. This was not about the pregnancy. It was not about insurance coverage. I was ready. We were both ready to take this final step.

After a lot of discussion regarding our preferences, we agreed to marry in a simple, intimate civil ceremony. Both of us had already participated in big, traditional weddings with our previous marriages. This ceremony was to exchange vows and commit ourselves to each other, not to put on a show. We chose a minister, and the ceremony was held at a local Italian restaurant. On March 22, 2014, my father, brother, his sister, and my boys joined our celebration. (My mother's health prevented her from attending.) I wore a lace, beige gown, and Giovanni wore his black suit. Afterward, we danced together to the Shania Twain song "From This Moment"—its lyrics truly described our relationship. My boys were happy for us.

After the delicious meal, I surprised Giovanni by singing the song "The Story" by Brandi Carlile. I wanted him to know how much he meant to me:

"All of these lines across my face, tell you the story of who I am.
So many stories of where I've been and how I got to where
I am.
But these stories don't mean anything when you've got no one
to tell them to. It's true, I was made for you.
I climbed across the mountain tops, swam all across the ocean
blue. I crossed all the lines, and I broke all the rules.
But baby I broke them all for you.
Oh, because even when I was flat broke, you made me feel like a
million bucks, You do. I was made for you.

You see the smile that's on my mouth. It's hiding the words that
don't come out. All of my friends who think that I'm
blessed, they don't know my head is a mess. No, they don't
know who I really am.
And they don't know what I've been through, like you do.
And I was made for you."

Giovanni accepted me for who I really was. He knew me—since our childhood and through my adult struggles. I was far from a perfect or great woman or mother, yet he loved me. He understood and accepted my intimate flaws and even loved me because of them. Even when I had nothing to offer him, he made sure that I understood that my love was all he needed.

Angela's Advice

All any one of us really needs from another person is true, honest love.

GABRIEL MADE A TOAST TO US. He spoke on behalf of himself and his brothers. He had truly become the big brother and male figure for them. My father toasted and blessed our day, as well. He was tearfully happy for us. This day was special and beautiful.

I continued to experience problems during my second trimester. I cramped constantly. Taking the stairs in our four-story house was very difficult. I took more breaks at work and kept my feet up to help the twins stay in longer. Every day, I faced a new challenge. I recalled a neighbor, Angela, had an acupuncture practice. I hired her to visit me twice a week. My sessions with her made a difference because the cramping diminished and allowed me to nap. She was my go-to throughout the pregnancy.

My obstetrician was useless. No exaggeration. I was admitted to the hospital with severe contractions at 21 weeks. The twins would be barely viable at this point, and I was taken to labor and delivery. The attendant called her, but she never returned the page. I was admitted overnight because I was dehydrated. (The dehydration was causing the cramps.) My obstetrician never called. I needed to find a new doctor.

I researched obstetricians affiliated with a Level IV Neonatal Intensive Care Unit (NICU) hospital. I prepared myself for the possibility the twins could be born premature. My older boys were all preemies, so I thought that the twins would be, too. While doing the research, I found a listing for Bradley classes. Although I had used guided imagery and Lamaze more than 20 years ago with the births of my boys, I needed a refresher, and Giovanni needed to learn about the birthing process. Bradley classes teach about natural childbirth, prenatal nutrition, relaxation for an easier birth, birth plans, and work with partners as coaches. I signed up. Weekly classes were held in the Upper West Side.

Traveling was growing harder for me, but I felt this class was important. Giovanni and I learned so much from Tanya, the instructor. She gave me obstetrician recommendations. We interviewed with a two-doctor practice called VOB in the Upper West Side. I fell in love with both of them at the meet-and-greet appointment. They were known as a high-risk specialty practice and had a very low cesarean section rate. (I feared a C-section, but knew that it could be my reality.) We signed on with them. Twice daily shots were still taking place, as well as weekly progesterone shots from nurse Shelley. Angela also was coming twice a week for acupuncture appointments. VOB recommended that I also see a reflexologist, Vera, on top of everyone I was already utilizing.

Vera was an incredible, highly-recommended woman who helped

ease my fears. Her work on me stopped the contractions more than once. She visited twice a week to work on me.

By this time, in my 26th week, I was ordered on complete bed rest. Peter completely took over the childcare. The parents had been made aware that my condition was extremely delicate. They wished me well. I trusted Peter to follow my lesson plans. I did the business paperwork from bed.

Jack and I were now speaking daily, since I had more free time. He wasn't feeling well. Jack had gone to a doctor, but he was vague about the diagnosis. He didn't want to worry me. Giovanni and I grew concerned about him because he was all alone except for his kids and ex-wife. Giovanni considered a trip to visit him, but my pregnancy stopped him from going. He wanted to be home in case the "Twinkies" were born.

Giovanni also had hired a handyman to finish the nursery in my dressing room. We were building a nursery next to our bedroom in my former dressing room. Laborers worked while I lay in bed, listening. Then Giovanni painted and installed flooring.

When I was 29 weeks pregnant, I experienced full labor contractions. Giovanni raced me to Mount Sinai hospital like a maniac, carefully but speedily, running the red lights, knowing the Twinkies' lives depended on it. I was quickly admitted and put on a magnesium IV to stop the contractions. The medicine felt like fire through my body at first but, slowly, it worked. I stayed in the hospital a couple days for observation.

The goal was to keep the twins inside me as long as possible. My support system was working overtime to ensure the Twinkies the best possible outcome. I got permission from my doctors to go to a play on Broadway, not only for my mental health, but also because my doctor was a big fan of Les Misérables. I was given a wheelchair to help me navigate the theater. This was my all-time favorite play, one I had seen several times, even at the Queen's Theater in England. I had my box of tissues ready on my lap when the curtain rose. It was a nice, short break from my bed rest, and I quickly returned to bed once home. I found myself happily humming a song of Les Mis: "One Day More." My body was helping to keep the Twinkies in utero every day. One day inside me meant one week less in the NICU.

I made it to 34 weeks, 34 and a half to be exact. On Friday, August 15, while Giovanni and I were watching a silly movie in bed, all of a sudden, my water broke. Water was everywhere. There was no confusion as to what had happened. Giovanni quickly drove us to Mount Sinai. We knew we were going to be twin parents that night. I was nervous and scared.

My obstetrician met us there. He assessed the situation and realized that Twin A was in distress. I was petrified. Every attempt by my acupuncturist, chiropractor, and reflexologist to move Twin A had been fruitless. Twin A's heartbeat had slowed down dramatically. I had no choice but to consent to a dreaded emergency C-section.

I do not remember the surgery, except in nightmares. Giovanni was present for the surgery, and he saw the twins briefly before they were quickly taken to the NICU. The twins' Apgar scores were 8 and 1. Apgar stands for "Appearance, Pulse, Grimace, Activity, and Respiration." In the test, these five items are used to check a baby's health. Each is scored on a scale of 0 to 2, with 2 being the best score. The twins were healthy. We were proud parents to Vincenzo and Caterina, our Twinkies.

I met the twins on Monday, three days after they were born. My poor health after the surgery had left me immobile for a few days. My oxygen levels lowered. I had trouble breathing. I hemorrhaged so much that I felt faint and weak from the blood loss. It took me a long time to recover from the trauma mentally, too. The drugs made me hallucinate and gave me horrible nightmares. The nightmares were so bad that they give me a muscle relaxer. I was a zombie then. (I am incredibly grateful to Giovanni for his loving, patient care that got me through that difficult time.) I had to get stronger to be allowed to travel down to the NICU.

Both babies were in incubators and very fragile. It felt strange to hold the twins. The connection was not immediate. I wondered whether they were actually mine! I realized this suspicion was insane but, still, I asked a nurse. She assured me that each child's name label had been attached to their legs at birth, and these security tags were never removed. I was familiar with this safety measure. These were not my first kids. I just needed the verbal assurance.

Time proved that Caterina was a mini-me. She was identical to my infant photos. Vincenzo was the spitting image of Giovanni. The parentage was obvious to our families.

The boys fell in love with their tiny siblings at first sight. My family had grown overnight. I was a mom of five children now.

The twins were admitted into the NICU as feeders and growers, meaning they needed to gain weight in order to be discharged. Caterina and Vincenzo weighed in at 4.7 and 4.11 pounds, respectfully. I had fully expected them to require oxygen, to be intubated, and to have nose feedings. Giovanni had prepped for this possible scenario, as well. We were surprised to find out the twins did not need these procedures. When I was discharged a week later, we traveled every day to see them in the NICU. I got into a routine: get up, work at the childcare, meet Giovanni after work, drive to Mount Sinai for the 6pm feeding, pick up dinner, another feeding three hours later and head home. Then, the long process would begin again the next day.

23

CIRCLE OF LIFE

GIOVANNI GOT A CALL DURING this time from Jack's ex-wife. He was hospitalized, and the doctors couldn't figure out what was wrong with him. First, we were told it was his heart. Jack had suffered a heart attack several years earlier. Next, we were told it was his liver, then his kidneys. I had no idea what was going on with him. His ex-wife had planned a family vacation to a beach destination several hours away. While she was away, Jack was transferred to another hospital in South Carolina. I was frantic. Jack was all alone. We got in touch with his ex-wife, and she cut her trip short. Jack was unresponsive, and his vitals were not strong.

In our car outside the NICU, I was finally connected by phone to Jack's hospital room. Jack experienced a brief surge of energy, and I was able to have one final conversation with him. He said, "Always love your husband and smile. Be happy. Forgive and love. Stand up for yourself. Be true to you. Stay strong. And be a friend to your boys now that they are older." Jack also asked me to check on his daughter.

I encouraged Jack to fight, not give up. I was not letting my friend go. His voice was barely a whisper on the phone. I was crying inconsolably. This was not a conversation I ever wanted to have with him.

His ex-wife showed Jack a photo of the twins. He blessed them. I was glad he saw them. I could not let myself believe what was happening. We were grounded in New York. We couldn't travel south with the Twinkies in the NICU. That was the last time I spoke with Jack. He died surrounded by his four incredible children and ex-wife on the evening of Sept. 1, 2014. I was crushed. It was the first time I lost someone I loved. I lost my best friend and confidant that night. It left me empty. I regretted the Twinkies would never meet Jack or know what a special man he was. I was determined to share stories about him as they grew up.

His ex-wife brought Jack up to New York to be buried alongside his mom and dad. We all attended Jack's funeral. Giovanni read a eulogy that was mostly written by me because I was closest to him. I poured my heart out in the eulogy for my friend who was gone too soon, leaving four remarkable children. To this day, I miss being able to pick up the phone and ask him for advice. I thank him for all the courage and strength he made me see I had inside.

After four weeks in the NICU, our Twinkies came home. I got into a routine and divided my time between caring for and nursing my newborns and working. Family came first, but the childcare was my responsibility, too. I needed to ensure everything ran smoothly because parents counted on me. I set up a playpen for my Twinkies in my office, so they could sleep while I worked. I was very busy and enjoying every moment.

My in-laws visited from Italy in September. They met their first grandchildren. They had never expected I would give them grandchildren. They felt very blessed. Vincenzo was named after his paternal great-grandfather. This made my in-laws very happy. Genoveva, now my mother-in-law, realized very quickly I was completely hands-on with the Twinkies. My experience with my own children and the 20

years of childcare showed in my care for the babies. I had more practice with children than anyone she knew.

With my first son Gabriel, I did not even know how to change his
diaper when he first came home from the hospital. I could have been
on *America's Funniest Home Videos* with him. First diaper change, his
diaper fell off. I used environment-friendly cloth diapers. It was a
disaster with a capital D. I had no clue how to nurse either. Thank
god, nursing is instinctual for babies, and Gabriel was good at it.
When he grew older, I boiled his bottles, like I had seen on TV, and
the bottles melted. Unfortunately, I had been very naive, and this
was before the internet.

Now with the Twinkies, I could swaddle one with one hand while
nursing the other. Caring for children was second nature to me.
Advice was given by me, not the other way around. My mother
wondered how I measured their intake because I was nursing. I
simply answered that I felt it, I noted their growth and their diapers
were wet during changes. My answers surprised her. (My mother
was not familiar with nursing.)

Giovanni and I had talked long and hard about the twins' future
while I was pregnant. I wanted them to be able to talk to their grandparents in their native languages. This meant that they needed to
learn English, Spanish and Italian. Consequently, I spoke to the
twins only in Spanish, Giovanni only spoke to them in Italian, and
they would hear English everywhere else. This adjustment was a
huge one for us. I usually only spoke Spanish to my parents, and
Giovanni usually only spoke Italian to his parents. This idea required
effort and consistency on our parts. I was extremely adamant that we
must make this idea work, so they could enjoy a multi-language
learning opportunity.

I had lost that opportunity with John because of his father. I was
a different person now, and I understood the value of speaking
different languages—more than ever.

* * *

Angela's Advice

Consider teaching your child other languages at a very early stage. The time range, from birth to 5 years, offers a fantastic window of opportunity to fill young synapses with languages.

* * *

GIOVANNI and I hosted a family reunion at our home in September. My parents, his parents, and my aunt and uncle (Giovanni's godparents) came over to meet the Twinkies. We took photos of all of us—together. Time was precious. Jack's sudden death had taught me that. We realized the significance and poignancy of hosting the six adults who had formed and supported us. I was very melancholy over Jack's death, and I saw this reunion as a final goodbye to the older relatives. My parents, Giovanni's parents, and my aunt Rosa and uncle Rafael would never be in the same room together again. Cherished memories.

Sadly, we were entering a stage when the gatherings with our extended families would be mainly for funerals. The birth of the Twinkies was the last birth in our generation. I was reminded of a situation from years earlier: Gabriel was newly born, and we were happily riding home from the hospital with him. A funeral procession drove past us, traveling in the opposite direction. Circle of life. With Jack's death and the Twinkies' birth, I was experiencing the circle of life firsthand.

Unfortunately, I did not have a village or family to help me raise my children in the past. I raised my older ones on my own for the most part. My parents and ex-in-laws were never involved. I was not counting on my parents now either as both were too elderly to help and I did not want disagreements. My in-laws lived in Italy, so I could not count on them. Now, I had twins and a full-time job. Luckily, this time around, my older boys became my village.

On the last day in September, Vincenzo choked on his vitamins and stopped breathing. He was lifeless and turning blue. I had to perform CPR to revive him. He was barely 6 weeks old. I held his tiny, 4-pound body in my hand and breathed into him. Tears rolled down my face while I breathed, counted and pressed. I worked methodically and prayed to all the gods to help me. I screamed for help between breaths. Performing CPR on your own child is not ideal. It feels more intense. Stressful. More pressure on me. (That is why doctors do not operate on their family members.) Because I was certified and had practiced CPR many times, I was able to resuscitate my own child.

I rushed Vincenzo out of the house and to the hospital when he started breathing again, leaving Caterina and the childcare with Gabriel, Peter and an assistant. My own family was chipping in when emergencies happened. I could rest assured the childcare was in good hands, too. Everyone at home was certified to work for me and I needed everyone now. Thankfully, EEG tests proved that Vincenzo was OK. This was an isolated incident and several days later, we were home.

The Twinkies were infected with RSV in November. Respiratory syncytial virus is a common respiratory virus that usually causes mild, cold-like symptoms. Most people recover in a week, but premature infants with RSV can wind up with pneumonia or bronchiolitis. This was a serious set-back for the twins. Luckily, I was able to stay with them while Peter managed the childcare. Gabriel would cover as a substitute along with another assistant. Vincenzo was intubated because his heart was strained and needed help. As a preemie, his lungs were not fully developed at birth. The doctor tried to tell me I needed to leave the room while they intubated my baby, but one look at my face told the doctor I was staying put and holding my child's hand through it all. I was no pushover anymore. I was his mother, and he needed me. Caterina fared better, not needing intubation, just breathing treatments.

Every day while I was in the hospital, I checked in with my staff (Peter, Gabe, and the assistant) to ensure everything was running smoothly. I still reviewed the lesson plans, reviewed their daily notes, and talked to the parents from the hospital. I used a private app to communicate with parents. I could communicate with the parents instantly. We had gone green—no more written daily logs. I used the app for sending nearly everything to the parents: menus, lessons, photos, and videos, among other notes on their children. It was very convenient.

My village was there for me. My boys wound up being very close to their much younger siblings, and their help allowed me to work in the childcare. I returned to work part-time for 5-7 hours daily until the twins were 6 months old. (After that, I worked full-time again, 40-50 hours weekly.) There was a protective air about my boys now. I felt it. Gabriel, Peter, and John were adults now, and they always wanted to make sure I was OK by checking in on me constantly. Our relationship had changed for the better. We listened to each other now. We honestly cared about each other. And the parents of the childcare loved Peter, too. The class called Peter "Teacher" now.

Laurie, my divorce lawyer, reached out to me in October 2014. She asked if I would be willing to give a speech about the work that PACE had done for me through my divorce. I agreed. It was the least I could do, considering the years and work she had put into my divorce. The speech was to be presented before the benefactors who made large donations. This money helped pay the legal fees for women in my situation or worse.

I was driven to the banquet hall in a limo. The attendees were formally dressed in tuxedos and gowns. Chandeliers hung from high ceilings, and a 10-foot water fountain was in the middle of the foyer. I mingled nervously. I had anxiety about speaking about my personal life in front of strangers. This speech held intimate details of my life and the circumstances surrounding my previous marriage. I was introduced, and I approached the podium. As I slowly read my speech, I started reliving the pain I had felt, which made me feel uneasy and hesitant to continue. The fear and vulnerability I felt during my marriage surfaced. I got choked up and needed to stop. Someone handed me tissues. My emotions were overflowing.

I had been a victim of emotional abuse. I finally accepted what I lived through, and now I was trying to relay how this type of abuse was often hidden—the scars and bruises were not visible to the naked eye. The soul was hurt. Most people are not aware that emotional abuse exists. They don't recognize it. I had been groomed not to recognize it myself.

I finished my speech with tears rolling down my face. The audience gave me a standing ovation. Many shook my hand afterwards and talked to me after my speech.

I was living proof that hurtful words and manipulations could erase a person. Four years earlier, I would not have believed that another life would be possible, but here I was, sincerely happy and loved. Previously, I had thought it was normal to be afraid to voice my feelings. I had thought it was normal to be degraded and manipulated. My thoughts and actions had been guarded all the time. My self-esteem had been slowly ripped apart. Now I was a completely changed woman. I was stronger. I was self-assured. I was finally happy—not because of my relationship or my business—I was happy with myself, who I was.

Somehow, despite all the pain and hardship my boys lived through with me, they came out OK in the end. My three sons became incredible young men, each leading different, fulfilling lives —respectable, honest, hard-working, reliable adults. Gabriel went into the health and fitness field as a master trainer. Peter worked with me as an early care educator and my right hand. John found his niche as a handyman. He helped complete many projects around the house. Gabriel was also my substitute as needed.

Although my three young men had their own lives, they remained in our home. We lived under one roof with our own spaces due to the unique setup of the house—four floors, each on a different floor. It was comfortable. (My adult children needed their privacy, and they got it.) We were close as adults, and we could count on each other. They each confided in me about personal matters, as well.

We had gone through a war and survived it. This made us stronger as a family unit. And my boys were protective of me, their mom and friend.

One night after work, Giovanni walked into the bedroom to find all three older boys, now men, stretched out on my bed, talking with me. They easily took over our bed. John was over 6 feet tall and easily stretched the length of the bed. Giovanni laughed at the sight and said to me: "You are lucky to have them all here with you. They love you and they like being with you."

24

NAFCC PROCESS AGAIN

IN 2016, I TOOK ON the self-study for NAFCC accreditation once again. This time I knew what to expect in many ways. The big difference now was this was a group family childcare, not a family childcare. This meant more children to care for, and my assistants needed to be vetted. It was not all about me anymore. First, I went through the standards on my own, then I held many staff meetings, covering each and every standard. It was not about simply passing to gain accreditation, but about embodying the standards, working them into our daily lives. It was a slow process because the Twinkies required my daily attention, too.

The standards had been updated since I had been accredited in Pennsylvania. They were still divided into five content areas: relationships, environment, development learning activities, safety and health, and professional and business practices. I asked my staff to self-assess carefully because they, as professional assistants, were specifically noted in the guidelines. We all needed to respectfully work together, show positive attitudes, be sincere and comfortable and enjoy our work. We all needed to be in the same boat, rowing in the same direction, so to speak. Despite our different personalities, we needed to share the same philosophy and code of ethics.

Peter was a loud, fun, spontaneous, people person and a natural with children. I was more laid-back, much quieter. I was also well organized. My other staff member at the time was similar to me in personality, and she followed our leads. Gabriel substituted for me or filled in when we needed an extra hand. Because he lived and worked from home, he was available at a moment's notice.

The environment standards were detailed. Are we organized? Is there enough room? Do we have a cozy space? Is heavy furniture anchored? We viewed the rooms through the children's eyes. We did not want overstimulation or under-stimulation. We ensured the childcare had sufficient supplies and safe materials and gross- and fine-motor development materials for all ages. Arrangement, spacing, lighting, shelving—all were reconsidered. I kept the standards in mind when I first set up the environment. Now, in the self-study process, we combed through each standard to ensure we were truly on task. I added more diverse books, puzzles, and dolls for cultural relevance. This time around, I had more than enough books, numbering more than 1,000 for the class. The developmental learning activities standard meant that a balance of child-directed activities and teacher-led activities occurred daily. Our schedules and routines needed to support the children's growth and development, allowing for ample time for free choice. The following are just some of the standards that we worked toward improving:

STANDARDS

NAFCC accreditation standard: Requires that the provider help the child and families to cope through separation anxiety.

I encouraged parents to stay as long as they wanted through a child's trial period and even after. To this end, I had a grandmother stay with us for more than five weeks all day, while her grandchild adjusted to her new environment and learning a new language. Separation anxiety impacted the new children and the first-time parents and grandparents. I would build a relationship with them, so they could trust me, and so their children could enjoy their time with me. Children picked up on their parents' hesitancy and fears. When their parents cried, children cried even more. I needed to be a place of comfort for all parties involved.

I realized how strong my relationships was with some families, such as previous clients from Pennsylvania. Luz, who helped me apply for health insurance for the boys, called me for advice. I had her girls in my care when they were barely 3 months and 18 months. Now, Alexandra and Janellie were 15 and 16 and wanted to volunteer with me. Seeing the girls all grown up made me proud. They called me their second mama because I had nearly raised them from infancy. (Now, these young ladies talked to me about their boy problems. Life goes on.)

NAFCC accreditation standard: The provider introduces cultural activities based on authentic experiences of individuals, rather than a tourist curriculum.

In order to incorporate a thorough look at different cultures, I invited parents to be part of international cultural month, which coincided with Month of the Young Child. I asked each parent to join the class on their own time schedules and share their cultures through music, food, stories, clothing, photos, and language. Even my husband came to class to tell the children about Italy. Giovanni showed the class a game to play, sang songs in Italian, read a book, and showed photos of Italy. Other parents taught the class how to dance salsa. Grandparents brought huge amounts of homemade dishes, and they shared stories from their cultures. We took this standard to another level with our inclusion.

Peter agreed to dress up for every holiday. As a class, we celebrated every holiday, very inclusively, with the parents' help. Peter became the Cat in the Hat for Dr. Seuss's birthday, a leprechaun for St. Patrick's Day, and even an elf for Christmas. We learned about holidays, such as Las Posadas and the Chinese New Year custom of giving money to children. I learned how to make latkes for Hanukkah. (A parent taught me how to cook them and told the children the story of the holiday.) Parents truly got involved with the class. Once given the opportunity, they wanted to participate. With full cooperation from families, holidays were not tourist-like but, instead, inclusive of all.

We also had great field trips to animal farms, nature centers, children's museums, and apple farms. Parents would caravan to the spots on the weekends and we would all have great fun. In addition, the parents shared the burden of supervising the children. (Because the parents drove their own children, I did not have insurance issues.) The parents also connected and networked with each other.

NAFCC accreditation standard: Children are engaged in large-motor activities for at least 30 minutes each half day.

The children's gym room, nicknamed "Monkeyville," was ideal for gross-motor play. They had a safe space to jump, climb, roll and run, in addition to dancing to music as part of the daily schedule.

* * *

Angela's Advice

Active children are happy children. Going outside every day to breathe fresh air and move around is essential for all children. Movement generates endorphins, which create a sense of happiness.

* * *

IN OUR CLASSROOM, there was a lot of movement and not a lot of "no." This was ideal. Ensuring that the environment is a second teacher made the days flow smoothly and easily.

NAFCC accreditation standards: Take the time for daily meaningful conversations with each child, regardless of age.

"Time" and "meaningful" were the keywords in this standard. I wanted to make sure each child felt comfortable with me and wanted to spend time in class. This required authentic effort with love and understanding. It could not be just the eye-catching fun stuff, but the heart-to-heart times too. I needed to make sure each child heard their name spoken frequently, not only when they did something wrong. Daily routines gave us time to speak to each child intimately, one on one. Diapering allowed for intimate, close conversations in a respectful manner. The child was asked and told about each step of the diapering process. During hand washing, we connected with each child. Lap time reading also was part of the day when the children were given the love and attention each one required.

Neurobiology, at its root, is all about connections. These are vital for the social, emotional health of little ones. Allowing the children to feel comfortable with all of us was key.

NAFCC accreditation standard: Children under the age of 3 are in the provider's line of sight at all times, except when she attends to personal needs for up to 5 minutes.

Having three staff members made fulfilling this standard easier. In Pennsylvania, I waited for the children to sleep during naptime before I used the bathroom. It was not ideal. (Trust me on that. It's hard when you really must pee, and you can't leave kids alone. Forget about when you have an upset stomach!)

Supervision had become a main concern with many centers because children had been lost during childcare hours. As a unit, we discussed how to ensure the class was accounted for at all times. We always knew the number of children present. When an inspector visited and asked, we could respond immediately. We never said, "Let me count, or let me check." We implemented a "magic number." The new magic number was created daily during the attendance check. During the parents' sign in, we clicked in each child in attendance using the app on our phones. On the whiteboard, we entered the magic number. We also frequently double-checked the attendance number throughout the day.

NAFCC accreditation standard: Children age 5 and under are not left inside or outside by themselves.

This standard was one of many that differed from New York state regulations. According to state regulations, providers can leave school-age children (meaning at least 5 years old) outdoors for 15 minutes at a time. The NAFCC standards required continuous, vigilant supervision, so I rightfully opted to fulfill the higher quality NAFCC standard. When I trained others regarding state regulations, I pointed out the difference in the supervision standards. I made sure everyone understood the NAFCC standard was to be followed for the safety of all the children.

Accidents happened. They have happened in front of me. Once my oldest son, at age 14, was playing soccer in the front yard. He kicked the ball and missed. In the process, he kicked a stone that cut his leg open. He limped inside to find me. His leg was gushing blood and we could see his bone. I applied pressure with a clean towel. Then, after I found a substitute, we left quickly for the ER. Gabriel required 19 stitches on his leg. There was no soccer season for him that year.

Another instance took place in front of four adults: my youngest Vincenzo, age 3, was kicking a soccer ball in my uncle's front yard. The ball rolled onto the pavement of the driveway instead of the grass. He kicked hard (Charlie Brown-style), missed, and fell backwards, cracking his head open. (OK, maybe soccer is not a good sport for my boys!) Vincenzo required three staples to his head. Four weeks later, his twin Caterina slipped backward on our child-size couch and banged her head. She had been sitting next to an adult when she slipped backwards. She had cracked her head, too! I took her to the ER, where she had three staples applied to her head. (These injuries were in the same areas of their heads. Twins—always mimicking each other!)

I could not think of leaving a child unsupervised for 15 minutes at any given time, regardless of age. (And my children's accidents happened in front of me or other adults.) My childcare children were under my supervision. I was hired by their parents to care for them. They trusted their little ones would be safe and stay healthy with me. If they had bumps or bruises, we were accountable. The last thing a parent wanted to hear was the staff did know how an accident occurred. We documented all incidents. Paper trails were important.

Without proper supervision, I would never have noticed that a 2-year-old had a seizure for the first time. I called her parents, and we took her to the ER. I spent the afternoon at the hospital, making sure the parents and child were OK. The physicians got the details of what happened firsthand. Supervision also meant listening to and watching the children's actions. I knew what was normal for each child. When they acted differently, something was up. Maybe they were feeling sick or tired. I watched for other symptoms, as well. I made sure to tell the parents everything I observed.

NAFCC accreditation standard: Children are not left in equipment that restrains their movements for more than 20 minutes at a time, except when eating or sleeping, and no more than half of the time in care.

Bouncers, swings, exercisers all take up a lot of space. I had seen childcares that have these restraint-type apparatuses throughout the room. It meant the little ones were moved from one stationary piece to another. I also witnessed little ones with flat and bald heads. This meant tiny humans were probably placed on their backs for long periods of time. I made sure all infant equipment, except for a high-chair and playpen for napping, were removed from the room. (I did not want "container babies.") This also cleared up space and got the little ones involved with the rest of the class at all times. Their freedom required a hands-on approach by all staff.

NAFCC accreditation standards: Poisonous items are locked in out-of-reach locations.

This standard made sense, obviously. I considered the mothers' purses hazardous—if they were anything like mine and filled with cosmetics (listed as poisonous items), pens (hazardous because of poking possibilities), and hand sanitizer (definitely a poison). Some moms smoked, so cigarettes and lighters could be found in their purses. Medications were another concern. I made a new rule: No purses were allowed inside the childcare. I advised parents to lock them in their cars.

NAFCC accreditation standard: If parents do not speak the language of the provider, the provider finds effective ways to communicate with them.

Living and working in New York meant interacting with various cultures in different languages, and I welcomed all into my program. In Pennsylvania, before the internet and smartphones, I used flashcards, interpreters, and sign language to communicate with parents. Now, I used Google Translate and my smartphone to translate instantly, promoting efficient communication with parents. Technology helped bridge the divide in communication. I also speak Spanish fluently and enjoy a basic understanding of Italian and French. I am also familiar with American Sign Language. This knowledge helped to communicate with families.

NAFCC accreditation standard: The provider implements an illness policy, defining mild symptoms with which the children may remain in care and more severe symptoms that may require notification of parents. Parents must have a back-up contact to pick up the child when they are not available.

MEDICAL POLICY/SHORT TERM (an excerpt from my program handbook. I used *Model Child Care Health Policies* published by The PA Chapter of the American Academy of Pediatrics and the American Academy of Pediatrics for reference.)

ADMISSION AND EXCLUSION

Children must remain home when they are sick. Do not bring your child in and hope that your child will get better throughout the day. A child MUST be kept at home at least 24 hours after a fever higher than 101 degrees or a severe upset stomach. Keep this 24-hour time-lapse in mind when bringing your child back to the childcare. This is a state law.

If a child becomes sick while in care at the facility:

1. Parents/guardians are notified immediately and are given a complete symptom record.
2. **Tue head teacher will determine whether the child may remain in the program or is too ill to stay in childcare.** In the case of a fever higher than 101 degrees or a severe digestive problem, the child must be picked up and may return after 24 hours if the fever has gone down and the child is feeling better. This is one way to protect the other children, preventing the rest of the children from getting sick. We ask that you bear this in mind. We ask that you use your best judgment when bringing in your child if you think that he/she may be getting ill.
3. Back-up childcare must be made available by the parent or guardian if the parent/guardian is unable to come and pick up their child. This person must be made aware of their responsibility in the case that your child may become sick while in care. This person must be authorized and be signed-off by the parent/guardian for the release of your child.
4. The symptom record will be shared and discussed with the parent/guardian so that all information needed to continue the child's care is maintained. If necessary, the teacher and parent/guardian will consult with the child's health provider for management of the child's illness.
5. The childcare is not a sick-care place. If your child is sick, keep them home or make other arrangements. The head teacher cannot be asked to provide individual care for a sick child all day when lessons and activities must be provided and the rest of the group must be supervised.

NAFCC accreditation standard: The provider gives parents receipts upon payments of fees or fees are fully subsidized. Also, the provider gives parents her Social Security number or Employee Identification Number with the first receipt and upon request.

When I first started the business in 1999, everything was manual. It was very tedious and time-consuming to write receipts and keep a paper accounting log. Now, I performed my bookkeeping utilizing the CACFP's KidKare system for my invoices, expenses, and deductions. I loved the convenience. I had no invoices to mail because they were automatically sent. End-of-year statements for parents were just a click away. My accountant easily reviewed all my reports.

I received an email from a client who needed a statement of account when I was out of the country. I was able to log into my account from abroad and send her the information with just a click. Simple, efficient, and professional.

NAFCC accreditation standard: The provider gathers information about the children and their families, such as special needs, fears, food preferences and important holidays and traditions, and updates the information as needed.

My enrollment interview and process became very detailed regarding each child's individuality in order to provide the best care for each child. In this book's appendix, there are some of the forms that I required to enroll into my program. These include a preliminary questionnaire, a family questionnaire (background information on each child), and much more.

NAFCC accreditation standards: Diapering areas must be separate from food areas.

I was very grateful for two bathrooms on the childcare floor. One was large enough for a changing table to fit inside of the tub. In the bathroom, I kept bins labeled with each child's name, and I stored their extra clothes, diapers, and wipes. The setup was ideal. My living space was not mixed with the childcare space whatsoever anymore. A separate entrance allowed privacy for my family. Now that my boys were adults, the privacy was nice. The Twinkies had their own areas in the main house with a den and playroom with their own toys. After dinner cleanup, the twins would go down to their home.

NAFCC accreditation standard: I must support a parent's choice to nurse and offer a place for this on site.

My attitude and hospitality made this childcare space very comfortable and accommodating. One year, five nursing moms gathered in a quiet, reserved space, talking and nursing and building their own network of friends and support systems. The five mothers nursed their little ones after a childcare party on the floor of the classroom. I was proud I made this possible for them. (Nursing is demanding, and the little ones need their moms for nutrition and comfort.) I had nursed all my own children as well, so I was very conscious of the occasional difficulties and the wonderful bonding moments.

My professional and business practices continued to excel. I was required to advance my training and education in family childcare and early care. This training was something I wanted for myself anyway. The training requirements, CEU's (Continuing Education Unit), and clock hours were recorded in my training log and portfolio. By going to conferences and taking courses, I learned more about my field. I wanted to be up-to-date with topics related to quality childcare. I attended workshops that were current with licensing regulations at my local childcare council.

I held parent workshops after hours on topics from first-aid basics to respectful parenting. I also hosted training sessions for other providers on topics ranging from contracts and policies to science and literacy.

My family handbook and contracts were updated and revised frequently. I held parent-teacher conferences to ensure everyone understood when changes were implemented to my policies. Example: An increase in tuition and registration fees and a new art/activity fee. (Art supplies and toys need to be replenished, and the cost could be prohibitive.)

I had tried to offset expenses with fundraisers. However, few parents had participated in these events and I had hardly gained any returns. An art-supply fee, twice a year, helped to defray the costs of supplies. I implemented a registration fee, as well, because parents sometimes toured my program, then said that they wanted to register. A space would be reserved for them, but they dropped out at the last minute. A nonrefundable registration fee reflected their true commitment to my program.

The business part of this job was not an afterthought anymore. In order for parents to view me as a professional during the interview, I was professional, and I clearly answered all questions about policies. In addition, I had references ready. My written policies covered topics such as emergency plans, illness, guidance, developmental activities, and parent participation. I reviewed each topic with each family during their interview, so all questions were answered and discussed.

My staff and I not only studied the standards, but we also read childcare books and articles. As a group, we studied and talked about current, respectful ways to speak to children, how to handle challenging behaviors, how to identify normal child development, and what to expect during the different stages of development. Understanding the children helped us do our jobs better. It was a matter of understanding that an 18-month-old would lack verbal skills to communicate fully when they were upset, nor would they have impulse control. Their behavior was put into perspective. Crying was treated respectfully, not dismissively.

Separation anxiety was something real and very emotionally painful to little ones. Our loving reaction to their behaviors helped them cope through all their difficult experiences.

The literature I assigned to my staff helped us go beyond the standards. We became a solid, strong, effective unit, working with children every day.

I wanted my staff to look professional, as well, so I bought polo shirts with the childcare logo on them to wear to work. I also bought sweatshirts with the same logo for the winter months. For work, I always wore a teacher apron. Professionalism was something we showed in our appearance, manner, speech, and knowledge. I aimed at making sure we were all professional.

Science Room

Science Room

Gym Room

Gym Room

Literacy Room

Block Area

Dramatic Play Area

Art Area

Ball Ramps

Music Area

My children, the loves of my life

All 5 kids John holding Vincenzo, Gabriel (oldest) holding
Peter and Caterina

Giovanni and Me

25

CHILDCARE OF THE HIGHEST QUALITY

W E SUBMITTED THE SELF-STUDY in late fall 2016, and the observer came shortly after. We had a normal day. There was no pretense about our work. We were authentic in our play with the children. The class understood what was expected of them and followed the usual daily schedule. Through our words and actions, we demonstrated what our work meant to us. When the observer left, Peter turned to me and said, "Well, that was simple!" It did seem simple because we had everything in place. We had studied for years and had fulfilled the requirements. We had worked together efficiently, smoothly and naturally. We knew our work and were confident with it.

In March 2017, we got the envelope with our NAFCC accreditation. I went to my bedroom, sat down, and just stared at the certificate. I took it in slowly. My husband walked in and observed me staring off into space. He saw the certificate in my hands and smiled. "You did it! I knew you would." He never doubted for one second when I had closed my business in PA that I could restart my business and become accredited again. I had never thought it possible. His faith and trust in that idea helped move me forward.

Giovanni was not familiar with the standards, but he knew me and just knowing me was enough. He had confidence I would accomplish what I wanted to. I was very grateful to my staff for accomplishing the accreditation, as well. Without their help, it would not have been possible. I made sure to give them a nice bonus to show my appreciation.

This accreditation meant more to me than it had in Pennsylvania. My struggle to get here had been arduous. I had learned the pain of loss and grown from it. I had learned to appreciate life even when I had nothing left. My journey to get here made me a stronger and confident woman. I was self-assured. There was no trace of the woman I was back in Pennsylvania. I was a professional. In addition, I was the first accredited group childcare provider in my county. I had done it again.

I led a life balanced between work and family. I had learned that balance was important to me. I looked in the mirror, into my eyes. The hurt and pain had been replaced by peace and love.

The childcare council of my county asked me to offer trainings. I trained other teachers—nights and weekends—and became their mentor. I did trainings at conferences. I also expanded my repertoire of trainings by offering workshops in Spanish. My life became more about childcare than it had in the past. I now served as a secretary on the leadership team for the regional AEYC Board. I was on the advisory board with PBS and gave my input on different projects. My work had expanded, and I loved it. This was who I was meant to be from the beginning.

26

NO MASKS

I REALIZED MY HEALTH HAD taken a beating, and I needed self-care. I listened to my body now. I took time for manicures, getting my hair done, enjoying walks, reading good novels, or just taking a nap. These were not luxuries. I had taken myself for granted too long. Self-care made me a better person, a better teacher and mother. I learned that I came first in order to be a better person for everyone around me. I learned to love me.

I enjoyed going to the gym early in the mornings on a regular basis—not so much for weight loss (although with Giovanni's delicious cooking, I had gained some weight) as much as strength building. I wanted my body to get stronger. After the gym, I would wake up my husband for work and get the Twinkies ready for class. I also found my quiet place, visiting Jack's grave. It was my spot for meditation. I will always miss him and think of him often.

I had a few new special friends now—a select few whom I called my friends. We called and texted and met up for lunches or dinners or a night out. We made plans individually or with our families. I remembered—all too well—not having someone to share life's ups and downs. I was not alone anymore in any sense. My house was filled with noise, love, all my boys and their respective friends, and my Twinkies. On the weekends, friends and cousins would hang out in my home.

Our lives were busy and, although we all lived together, we sometimes missed each other during the day because our schedules differed. In order to keep in touch with each other, I instituted a family dinner every Sunday night. These dinners were noisy—three or four conversations going on at the same time. We each tried to get in a word. Food platters were passed around several times. The love and affection we felt for each other was obvious during these meals.

Recently, I sent a text to a very good friend. I had met her at an NAFCC conference. (Best friends and networking happen there.) I sent her a song called "You Can Count on Me" by Bruno Mars. There was no special reason that day to send her the song. I was just letting her know that I was thinking of her. Life was too precious and short not to tell her that I cared about her.

27

MY CURRENT LIFE

S INCE MOVING FROM PENNSYLVANIA, MY life has taken a turn for the better. I have an amazing, loving, hard-working husband. We are partners in every sense of the word. The fact that we are *not* novices at relationships helps to make our marriage work. We both remember well what we had before and love what we have together now. Respect and love are the building blocks of our lives. Trust binds us together. We experienced a lifetime of pain in the short time that we have been together, which made us stronger as a unit, and we look forward to the future with hope and love.

I thank Giovanni for helping me to get me where I am. Giovanni says I would have gotten here without him. He may be right, but having a partner and friend who supports and encourages me makes a huge difference. I am not perfect in any way, shape, or form, but I am resilient. I honestly never believed that I could become a modern-day Job, yet, that is what happened. I lost everything only to be granted so much more than I ever imagined, including an incredible husband and loving children.

Life is like a chessboard. We are pieces in the game of life. Every move we make, every decision leads to another move. I lost a lot of pawns during my game, but I was able to retain my main players, my children. To that end, my boys are very open with me and seek my advice. I am proud of them, and I love my entire family dearly.

One day, not too long ago, John said, "You did good, Mom. You did good. We made it." This acknowledgment makes me happy. I am pleased to know he feels this way. Each one of the boys has made similar statements to me since we all moved back in together.

My first husband enjoys birthday dinners with us as well, bringing along his wife and beautiful daughter. We are *all* family, and time has taught us that we need to be there for each other. My family and children will always be the center of my life. I am thankful for them.

Make a point of telling your children that you love them every single day. Let friends and relatives know that you love them every time you think of them—text, call, email. Live with awareness every day because we only have the present, and the future is completely uncertain. Our lives are our own to make the best of—one day at a time. Never ever give up hope. As Tim McGraw sings: "Live like you are dying." I do.

I hope at least one person reading my story can gain strength from it. I also hope this reader understands each day can be better than the day before. Trust me: I was knocked down hard, but I came back, and so can you. Each of us experiences our own ups and downs during life's journey. Mine led me to children and childcare. Your life may take you in any direction you choose.

I look forward to my future—its endless possibilities—and so should you.

APPENDIX

Here are a few forms I created or recreated from helpful websites. These forms are essential for the business side of childcare. Contracts and policies need to be completely filled out and signed, keeping all matters clear. A checklist offers an outline of forms I require for enrollment. Feel free to use these forms in your childcares.

CHECKLIST OF FORMS TO BE COMPLETED

Name of child: _____

_____ Interview questionnaire (completed during initial conference)

_____ Copy of insurance card

_____ Copy of birth certificate

_____ Ages and stages screening permission form

_____ Child and Adult Food Program, CACFP (food program application)

_____ Childcare health assessment (completed prior to enrollment by physician)

_____ Childcare agreement/contract

_____ Consent for program activities

_____ Consent for photo/video

_____ Emergency contact form (blue form required by the state of New York)

_____ Family/holiday questionnaire

_____ Medical policy

_____ Napping permission form

_____ Topical permission form

_____ Termination policy

_____ Childcare protection policy

_____ Biting policy

_____ *Special care plan (if applicable)

_____ *Asthma/healthcare plan

_____ *Custody papers (if applicable)

_____ *Subsidy application (if applicable)

_____ *Translation service form (if applicable)

_____ 4-by-6 photo of your child

Reviewed by: _____

Date: _____

Registration fee: _____

Art/activity fee: _____

Tuition: _____

Days/time of care: _____

Referred by: _____

ABC Child Care
123 Lane
Anytown, USA

PRELIMINARY QUESTIONS:

Child's name _____

Date of birth _____

Date _____

Parent/guardian name _____

Contact number_____

Email _____

Address_____

Parent/guardian name _____

Contact number_____

Email _____

Address_____

1. Does your child have any siblings? _____
    What are their ages? _____
    How do they get along? _____

2. Do you have any pets? _____
    If so, what kind?_____
    Does your child have any fears or allergies to pets? _____

3. How do you describe your child's temperament? _____

4. Who will be dropping off or picking up your child?_____

5. When was your child's last physical?_____
    Are all immunizations up-to-date? _____

6. How do you describe your child's health? How often has your child been sick
    this past year?_____
    What were the illnesses? _____
    Is there any medical history I should know about?_____
    _____

7. Do you have back-up care if your child becomes sick or is your job flexible? _

    _____

8. Have there been any significant changes in your child's life recently? _____

    _____

    _____

9. Parent/guardian, where are you employed? _____

    What is your occupation?_____

    What are you hours and days of work?_____

    What holidays are you off from work? _____

    _____

    Are you able to be called at work when your child is too sick to remain in childcare? _____

    Hours and days of care requested? _____

10. Parent/guardian 2, where are you employed? _____

    What is your occupation?_____

    What are you hours and days of work?_____

    What holidays are you off from work? _____

    Are you able to be called at work when your child is too sick to remain in childcare?_____

    Hours and days of care requested? _____

11. If applicable, what does your childlike/dislike about their previous provider?

    _____

    _____

    _____

SCHEDULE

1. Describe your child's schedule at home? (eat, nap, play outdoors)_____
   _____
   _____
   _____
   _____
   _____
   _____

2. What does your child like to eat? _____
   _____
   _____
   What foods do they dislike? _____
   _____
   _____

3. If applicable, do they have special nap-time routines or items that comfort
   them? _____
   _____
   _____

4. Has your child been involved with another daycare before? _____
   Was this experience recent?_____
   Was this experience pleasant? If not, why not? _____
   _____

5. What are your current goals for your child? _____
   _____
   _____
   _____
   _____
   _____

PROGRAM ACTIVITIES AND DISCIPLINE

1. How does your child like to spend the time? _____
   _____
   _____
   What toys do they like? _____
   What activities do they like to do? _____

2. What types of discipline do you use at home? _____
   _____
   _____
   What do you do when your child misbehaves? _____
   _____

3. Would your child manage well in a mixed-age group setting?_____
   _____
   _____

4. What is your feeling about TV watching?_____
   How much TV does your child watch at home? _____
   *(Note that we do not use any TV in class. Use of iPads or tablets is strictly
   supervised and restricted to educational programs)*

5. Are there any special precautions about being outdoors? _____
   _____
   _____
   Are there special things you do to keep your child safe? _____
   _____
   _____

6. How do you feel about gun play? *(Note no gun play/water guns allowed at this
   facility)* _____
   _____

Any other special notes you would like us to know: _____
   _____
   _____
   _____
   _____
   _____
   _____
   _____
   _____

ABC CHILD CARE AGREEMENT

This contract is between:
Provider/Teacher:
Name: _____
Address: _____
Phone: _____

And

Parent/Legal Guardian
Name: _____
Address: _____

Phone: _____
Email: _____

Parent/Legal Guardian:
Name: _____
Address: _____
Phone: _____
Email: _____

For the care of:
Child's name: _____
Date of birth: _____

I, _____, the legal guardian of _____
agree to the following policies and rules of this facility by signing this agreement form.

— Understand that my child will be cared for as described in parent/guardian handbook.
— I can expect to have updates on my child's progress daily (through verbal communication and written notes on file), daily through communication reports via the app, twice a year through developmental checklists and through parent-teacher conferences.
— Daily class reports will be given in the daily notes through email via the app.
— Monthly newsletters and calendars will offer updates on coming events.
— Agree to meet with the teacher at least once a year or as needed for a conference to discuss progress, development and vital information regarding my child's care at this facility.
— Nursery/preschool age-appropriate creative curriculum will be provided as part of tuition and is described in the parent handbook.
— Pay the fee of _____ per week/day/hour (circle one)_____

If part-time, state what days are requested for care: _____
(Part-time scheduled days are set and not interchangeable.)

— Pay **the one-time nonrefundable registration fee of $300** at enrollment time.
— Enrollment procedures:
— Interview
— Review handbook
— Registration fee/forms filled out/checklist complete
— Getting to know time
— Trial time for three weeks
— Final enrollment conference
— In lieu of any fundraisers, ABC Child Care charges the **activity/art fee of $100** at the start of care and then twice annually in February and September.
— Child's normal arrival time _____
  Child's departure time _____
— Note that if pick up is after closing time, there is a **late fee of $15 per every 15-minute increment after 7 pm.**
— Call the director or staff by 9 a.m. if my child will be out for any reason or late arriving in the morning.
— I will notify the director if I will be late picking up my child, unless it is an emergency. (Staff need to be made aware they would be working longer hours.)
— Pay in cash on Monday or the first day of the week for child for the first three weeks during the trial period. After that, payments are then made payable the week prior to care with the first week overlapping with the last cash payment. **Payment methods: online, PayPal or cash on Monday or first day of care.**
— Pay late fee of **$20** per day payment is made past due date.
— Understand that if I go **beyond the 60 hours** a week of care, there is an **extra charge of $15 an hour.**
— I have been given a copy of the family handbook and understand the policies and procedures.
— I will follow policies and regulations in family handbook to the best of my ability.
— If I have any questions about the policies, I will ask the director.
— I understand if the policies and regulations are not followed and I've being reminded during a conference, it can be cause for termination from childcare.
— I understand the termination policy and received a copy of it in the handbook.
— I will obtain a special care plan if applicable, in conjunction with my child's healthcare provider.
— I will obtain a health assessment for my child, according to the schedule recommended by the American Academy of Pediatrics.
— Notify the director when my child is scheduled for routine health visits, obtain a form, complete it and return it.
— Cooperate with the program and child's healthcare provider to follow up on any medical and dental and developmental needs of my child.
— Notify the staff when my child is ill or when any family member has a contagious disease.
— I understand and will follow all the medical procedures and sick care policy of this facility. If my child is sick, I will not bring he/she into class.
— If my child needs a doctor's note to return to class, I will obtain it prior to bringing my child back.
— I will complete a medication consent form when requesting medication administration, including over-the-counter medications.
— I understand the director does not supply medication or administer medication without my written and verbal consent.

— Notify the director in advance if I plan to have a birthday party for my child at the preschool.

— I understand I can participate in the program through many ways, such as:
- party involvement
- story time
- special occasions
- class trips
- bringing in healthy snacks
- contributing to classroom activities
- sharing career/travel/vacation experiences
- donating items (i.e. books, recyclables)
- preschool get-togethers
- input to director about any improvements

— Provide the program with the necessary items needed for my child's care as described in the handbook and other items my child may need. If this is not provided, I understand that my child **may not** be left in daycare. Daycare does not provide "items needed" as stated in program book.

— Items needed: (check off those needed) All items must be clearly labeled with your child's name.
- complete set of change of clothes (note your child's growth and weather)
- a smock or old shirt for painting
- sippy cup or individual cup
- a sleeping bag and/or two blankets
- a playpen for sleeping (if child is under 2)
- diapers and wipes and creams (if applicable)
- bottles (if applicable)
- slippers (if used)
- hairbrush or comb and hair accessories (circle if applicable)
- hats (summer)
- bibs (if necessary)
- sunblock lotion

— Provide information on how to be contacted in an emergency, which I will update when it changes and every six months.

— Understand the **__paid vacation__** schedule follows all federal holidays including:
- New Year's Day
- Martin Luther King, Jr. Day
- Presidents' Day
- Good Friday
- Easter Monday
- Memorial Day
- July 4th
- Labor Day
- Columbus Day
- Veterans Day
- Thanksgiving
- Day after Thanksgiving

— If a holiday falls on a Saturday, then it is observed on Friday. If a holiday falls on Sunday, then it is observed on Monday.
— This facility has three weeks paid vacation time. I understand during the first two weeks of August and week between Christmas Eve and New Year's Day this facility is closed.
— Understand all tuition payments are due prior to any vacation/closures.
— I understand the director will try to arrange for substitute care to avoid personal/sick days, but, if not available, then I am responsible for back-up childcare at my own cost.
— I will inform the director of my own vacation schedule two weeks ahead of time.
— Tuition payment is due prior to hiatus period/sick period/or vacation time. **Tuition payment remains the same regardless of attendance.**
— There is a <u>blackout period</u> between June 10 and August 16. Termination or conclusion of childcare must be done before then if your child is not going to stay for the month of August. No termination of care is done during summertime. Arrangements must be made beforehand for transitioning. If you do leave during the blackout period, tuition payment will remain in effect until Aug. 16.
— Understand that Angela Bayer-Persico is a mandated reporter and will report any case of suspicions of child abuse or neglect to Child Line directly or to Children and Youth services directly and follow their directives.
— I understand as the parent/guardian, I will be held liable for outstanding tuition payments and I can be taken to court if payments are not fulfilled. Legal fees would be paid by the parent/guardian.
— Agree to discuss my concerns with Angela Bayer-Persico.
— Notify the director if anyone else will be picking up my child.
— Designated persons to whom my child may be released to are: _____
  _____
  _____

By signing, you are agreeing you have read and understand and agree to adhere to these policies and procedures.

Print legal guardian name: _____
Signature _____
Date_____

Print legal guardian name: _____
Signature _____
Date_____

Print director/provider name: _____
Signature _____
Date_____

ABC Child Care
123 Lane
Anytown, USA

PERMISSION FOR AGES AND STAGES SCREENING

Child's name _____

Date of birth _____

Date _____

Parent/ guardian name _____

Contact number _____

Email _____

Address _____

I, _____, give permission for staff at ABC Child Care to use the Ages and Stages screening tool to assess my child. I will receive a copy of these assessments as they are completed and complete the parent portion of these assessments. This will help provide the best quality of care for my child.

The information will be used solely to plan and coordinate the care of my child and will be kept confidential and may only be shared with _____ (name of staff).

Parent name _____   Date _____

Parent's Signature _____   Date _____

Staffname_____   Date _____

CONSENT and RELEASE FOR CHILD
TO BE PHOTOGRAPHED and/or VIDEO TAPED

Name of facility: _____

Address of facility: _____

Name of child: _____

Consent is given for the following items initialed below:

_____   Private Facebook

_____   Website

_____   Photo journals

_____   Class albums

Legal guardian's signature _____

Date _____

Provider's signature_____

Date _____

CONSENT FOR CHILD CARE PROGRAM ACTIVITIES

Name of Facility: _____

Address of Facility: _____

Name of Child: _____

Consent is given for the following items initialed below:

- Walks around facility premises.
- Free play outside weather permitting (25 degrees to 95 degrees, no rain/snow)
- Planting, and weeding vegetables and flowers.
- Age appropriate art activities.
- Age appropriate science experiments.
- Cooking and baking under adult supervision.
- Homework supervision
- Participate in the daily curriculum plans for the day as per handbook.
- Participate in iPad or tablet under supervision for educational purposes
- Allow facility to obtain medical care for my child as deemed necessary.
- Allow teacher to take photos and film my child for teaching purposes and record keeping for photo journal.
- Allow director to give my phone number and address to prospective clients

Legal Guardian's Signature

_____

Date

_____

Legal Guardian's Signature

_____

Date

_____

Provider's Signature

_____

Date

_____

ABC Child Care
123 Lane
Anytown, USA

SLEEPING/ NAPPING ARRANGEMENTS

Child's name: _____

Date of birth: _____

Date: _____

Parent/ guardian name:

Contact number: _____

My child has my permission to sleep in the following rooms of the home: _____
_____

My child has my permission to sleep on: crib   mat   bed (circle one)

I understand that sleeping arrangement for infants require that the infant be placed on his or her back to sleep, unless I provide medical information to the provider that shows that arrangement is inappropriate for my child.

I do   I do not   (circle one) give my permission for my child to nap or sleep in a room where an awake adult is not present. I understand that the doors to all rooms must be open, the caregiver must remain on the same floor as the children and functioning electronic monitor must be used in any room where children are sleeping and an awake adult is not present

I do   I do not   (circle one) give my permission if my child is in evening or night care to allow the caregiver to sleep while my child is sleeping.

I understand that if my child is not able to nap, that time and space will be provided for quiet play and that my child will not be forced to rest for long periods of time

Signature of parent or guardian _____

Signature of provider _____

ABC Child Care
123 Lane
Anytown, USA

FAMILY QUESTIONNAIRE

Child's name _____

Date _____

1. Who are the primary caregivers for your child? _____

2. What is the household composition? _____

3. What holidays do you celebrate as a family? _____
   _____
   _____

   Note: This facility celebrates all holidays in order to be inclusive including, but
   not limited to, Dr. Seuss Day, Fourth of July, Memorial Day, Thanksgiving,
   Chanukah, Christmas, Kwanzaa and Presidents' Day.

4. Are there special or cultural traditions that you observe as a family? (beading,
   piñatas …) _____
   _____
   _____

   Would you be willing to share these traditions with the class? (Examples: bring in a
   book, share photos with the class or cook food for the class.) _____
   _____
   _____
   _____

5. What special foods do you and your family members prepare and eat? (empanadas,
   challah, dumplings …) _____
   _____
   _____

6. Would you be willing to make food for the class? _____
   _____
   _____

7. Do you speak more than one language? If so what? _____
   _____
   Would you be willing to teach the children a few words in this language? _____
   _____

8. How would you describe your child's ethnicity? _____
   _____

9.   Do you know any traditional stories typical of your background?_____
     _____
     _____

10.   If so, would you be willing to share them? _____
      _____

11.   Is there any other information that you would like us to know about your child's
      background to help us understand your child better? _____
      _____
      _____
      _____
      _____

ABC Child Care
123 Lane
Anytown, USA

TERMINATION POLICY FORM

The contract/agreement will be considered terminated if any of the following occur: (Unless otherwise noted, two-weeks' notice must be given.)

1. Non-payment exceeding three days (note that late charges are added). <u>Immediate termination.</u>
2. A continuous pattern of paying tuition late after being reminded of tuition payment time. Discretion is left up to director. Termination is with one-weeks' notice if paid for week, otherwise, <u>immediate.</u>
3. Absence exceeding three days without any notification. <u>Immediate termination.</u>
4. Discipline problem continues after parent conference.
5. Termination is <u>immediate</u> if child shows **intentional** violent behavior.
6. If the director or parent decides to terminate service, a two-week courtesy notice is required.
7. At the end of the three-week trial period, the director or parent may terminate service in the best interest of the child—<u>immediately.</u>
8. If the child's daily care requires more care than the childcare staff is able to provide and compromises the needs of the other children in the group.
9. If, after one warning, the parent or guardian does not follow the program's policies and regulations contained in this facility's handbook.

_____

Child's name

_____   _____

Parent/guardian   Date

_____

Provider signature

REFERENCES

The National Association for Family Child Care, (2004). Accreditation Health and Safety Guidebook.

Aronson, S. S. (2014). Model Child Care Health Policies. *Elk Grove, IL; American Academy of Pediatrics.*

APHA Press, imprint of American Public Health Association. (2019). Caring For Our Children: National Health And Safety Performance Standards: Guidelines For Early Care And Education Programs. *Washington, DC.*

Copple, C. & B. S. (n.d.). Developmentally Appropriate Practice in Early Childhood Programs.

Washington D.C.: National Association for the Education of Young Children.

PLF Press

Made in the USA
Columbia, SC
19 May 2021